THROUGH FIVE ADMINISTRATIONS

REMINISCENCES OF
COLONEL WILLIAM H. CROOK
BODY-GUARD TO PRESIDENT LINCOLN

ABRAHAM LINCOLN

From the original negative taken from life by Brady in 1864, now in the private collection of Frederick H. Meserve, New York City.

THROUGH FIVE ADMINISTRATIONS

REMINISCENCES OF
COLONEL WILLIAM H. CROOK
BODY-GUARD TO PRESIDENT LINCOLN

COMPILED AND EDITED BY
MARGARITA SPALDING GERRY

ILLUSTRATED

HARPER & BROTHERS PUBLISHERS
NEW YORK AND LONDON
MCMX

Copyright, 1907, 1910, by HARPER & BROTHERS

Copyright, 1908, 1909, by THE CENTURY CO.

Copyright, 1910, by THE CURTIS PUBLISHING COMPANY

Published October, 1910.
Printed in the United States of America

ISBN: 978-1-6673-0529-5 paperback
ISBN: 978-1-6673-0530-1 hardcover

CONTENTS

CHAP.		PAGE
I.	LINCOLN AS I KNEW HIM	1
II.	THE WHITE HOUSE FAMILY AND OTHER PEOPLE	14
III.	THE ENTRANCE INTO RICHMOND	38
IV.	A NEW PHASE OF THE ASSASSINATION	60
V.	ANDREW JOHNSON IN THE WHITE HOUSE	80
VI.	DISSENSION WITH THE RADICALS	96
VII.	THE IMPEACHMENT	112
VIII.	AFTER THE IMPEACHMENT	133
IX.	WHITE HOUSE UNDER U. S. GRANT	153
X.	FAMILY LIFE OF THE GRANTS	176
XI.	POLITICAL DISSENSION	189
XII.	RUTHERFORD B. HAYES IN THE WHITE HOUSE	222
XIII.	SOCIAL LIFE IN THE HAYES ADMINISTRATION	245
XIV.	GARFIELD AND ARTHUR	256

ILLUSTRATIONS

ABRAHAM LINCOLN	*Frontispiece*	
ABRAHAM LINCOLN	*Facing p.*	32
ANDREW JOHNSON		82
THE SENATE AS A COURT OF IMPEACHMENT FOR THE TRIAL		132
ULYSSES S. GRANT		154
RUTHERFORD B. HAYES		224
JAMES A. GARFIELD		258
CHESTER A. ARTHUR		276

THROUGH FIVE ADMINISTRATIONS

THROUGH FIVE ADMINISTRATIONS

I

LINCOLN AS I KNEW HIM

IT was in November, 1864, that four police officers were detailed by Mr. William B. Webb, who was then chief of police in the District of Columbia, to be a special guard for President Lincoln. They were to act on instructions from headquarters, and were also to be subject to any orders the President might give. The men were Elphonso Dunn, John Parker, Alexander Smith, and Thomas Pendel. All have since died. They reported immediately to the White House. Not long after the appointment a vacancy in the position of doorkeeper occurred, and the place was given to Pendel. On the 4th of January I was sent to the White House to act as the fourth guard.

. There was rotation in the service, although the hours were not invariable. The general plan was this: Two men were on duty from eight in the morning to four in the afternoon. These officers guarded the approach to the President in his office or elsewhere in the building, accompanied him on any walks he might take—in general, stood between him and possible danger. At four another man went on duty and remained until midnight, or later if Mr. Lincoln had gone outside the White House and had not returned by that time. At twelve the second night-guard went on duty, and remained until he was relieved, at eight in the morning. The night-guards were expected to protect the President on his expeditions to and from the War Department, or while he was at any place of amusement, and to patrol the corridor outside his room while he slept. We were all armed with revolvers.

The reasons why the friends of Mr. Lincoln insisted on this precaution were almost as evident then as they became later. Marshal Ward Lamon and Secretary Stanton had been begging him, it is reported, since 1862 not to go abroad without protection of some kind. Mr. Lamon is on record as having said that he was especially fearful of the President's showing himself at the theatre. He considered that a public place of amusement offered an opportunity for assassination even more favorable than Mr. Lincoln's solitary walks or the occasional drive or horse-back ride he took to the Soldiers' Home. Mr. Stanton is known to have been angered by a lack of caution which, on the part of a man so indispensable to the welfare of the nation as its President, he regarded as foolhardiness. For the President had always been inclined, in his interest in the thing that absorbed him, to forget that he was vulnerable. Every one remembers how, when he was watching Early's threatened attack on the fortifications north of Washington, he exposed himself recklessly to chance bullets. He hated being on his guard, and the fact that it was necessary to distrust his fellow-Americans saddened him. He refused to be guarded as long as it was possible for a sane man to persist.

But toward the end of 1864 so much pressure was brought to bear on him, particularly by Marshal Lamon and Secretary Stanton, that he finally yielded. He had admitted to Ward Lamon before this that he knew there was danger from a Pole named Garowski, who had been seen skulking about the White House grounds. He told Lamon of a shot that had barely missed him one day when he was riding to the Soldiers' Home. Conspiracies to abduct or assassinate the President were constantly being rumored. At first he contended that if any one wanted to murder him no precaution would avail. Finally, although he was always more or less of this opinion, the President gave way to the anxieties of those near to him. He consented to the daily guard of police officers, and, on longer journeys, to a cavalry guard.

There were many reasons why this fact was not known at the time and has not been generally understood since. In the first place, the President's bravery (rashness, some called it), was so universally recognized, he had refused for so long to take any precautions, that people were not looking for him to change. In the second place, both from his own feelings and as a matter of policy, he did not want it blazoned over the country that it had been found necessary to guard the life of the President of the United States from assassination. It was not wise—especially at this critical time—to admit so great a lack of confidence in the people. He was sensitive about it, too. It hurt him to admit it. But realizing that he had been chosen to save the country from threatened destruction, he forced himself, during the last months of his life, to be somewhat more cautious. When he had yielded, however, because of all these reasons, he wished as little show as possible of precaution. We wore citizen's clothes; there was no mention of the appointment in the papers or in official records; we walked with him, not behind him. The President was simple in his manners; he was in the habit of talking freely with any one who wished to speak to him. So it happened that a passer-by had no way of knowing that the man in plain clothes who walked by Mr. Lincoln's side was any other than the casual friend, office-seeker, petitioner, adviser, who helped to fill up every minute of the President's waking time.

I was very much surprised when the order came to report to the President for duty, and naturally elated. It was one Monday morning. I had never been inside the White House. I had seen Mr. Lincoln, and regarded him vaguely as a great man, but had never spoken to him. The first few days I was getting my bearings and accustoming myself to the new duties.

On the 9th I was put on night duty, covering the first part of the night. And so it happened that I was on guard at the first evening reception of the year, on the 9th of January. I knew the White House very well by this time—that is, the state apartments of the first floor and the President's office in the southeast corner up-stairs. The spectacle awed me at first. I had never seen anything like it before. The reception, or "levee," as the name was then, was crowded. It was generally considered a brilliant affair. I know it dazzled me.

The President and Mrs. Lincoln stood in the octagon Blue Room, near the western door. I was in the main entrance just outside, near where the broad flight of steps used to go up to the second floor. The guests entered the northern door, left their wraps in the cloak-rooms which had been constructed in the corridor, assembled in the Red Room, made their way to the Blue Room, where they were received. Then they progressed, greeting friends in the crowd, through the Green Room to the great East Room, where they remained. On the right of the President was Mr. John G. Nicolay, one of the two secretaries; on his left Deputy-Marshal Phillips. Commissioner French presented the guests to Mrs. Lincoln. I suppose I could hardly be expected to remember what the ladies wore. But my wife saw in the paper the next day that Mrs. Lincoln wore white silk trimmed with black lace. She had a wreath of white flowers in her hair, and wore a necklace of pearls. I suppose the costume, hoop-skirts and all, would look ugly to me to-day. But we all thought Mrs. Lincoln looked handsome. To my mind she was a pretty woman, small and plump, with a round, baby face and bright black eyes. Senator Sumner was present, and Senator Chase with a party. That reminds me of what was to me the most exciting moment of the reception.

My orders were to allow no one who wore wraps of any kind to pass into the Blue Room. The reason for this is not hard to find. Precautions against violence were being redoubled, and this was one of them. It would be the easiest thing in the world for a would-be assassin to smuggle weapons in under the voluminous cloaks then worn. It had been announced that guests were expected to leave their wraps in one of the rooms appointed for them. I had been instructed to make absolutely no exceptions. The newspapers the next day said: "The rule of decorum relating to wraps was very generally observed." They didn't know about my little experience.

Several guests had attempted to enter still wearing their cloaks. But no one resisted the order when it was made known. Finally a very handsome young woman came in who asked for Senator Chase's party. She wore a wrap that completely hid her dress. She could have brought in a whole arsenal of weapons under its folds. I told her that she could not enter until she left her cloak in the cloak-room. She became angry.

"Do you know who I am ?" she demanded, haughtily. I was rather nervous, for it was my first experience saying "Must not!" to White House guests. But I managed to say I did not know who she was.

"I am Mrs. Senator Sprague," she announced, as if that were final. I had heard of Kate Chase Sprague, of course, as had every one else in Washington, and of her father's ambition and her own brilliant career. But I tried to be courageous, and told her as politely as I could what my orders were and why they were given. When she saw the reason of the restriction she took off her cloak quite graciously and went in to meet her friends.

By this time most of the guests had arrived, so I had an opportunity to look about me. It was all bright and gay. For this evening at least there was no sign of the gloom that was pretty general throughout the city.

The people who crowded the rooms were in keeping with their brilliant character. The men were marked by a shade of extravagance in the cut and material of their evening clothes. There were many army officers in full uniform among the guests. The women looked like gorgeous flowers in their swaying, buoyed-out skirts. They were gayly dressed, as a rule, with the off-shoulder style of low-necked gown; they all wore wreaths of flowers in their hair. The general effect of the scene was brilliant.

About eleven the President, with Mrs. Dennison, the wife of the new Postmaster-General, on his arm, followed by Mrs. Lincoln escorted by Senator Morgan, entered the East Room. They talked for a few minutes with their guests and then retired—Mrs.

Lincoln to her own room and the President to the library up-stairs. The levee was supposed to be over at eleven, but some people remained until nearly twelve. After they had all left, Mr. Lincoln wrapped himself in the rough gray shawl he usually wore out-of-doors, put on his tall beaver hat, and slipped out of the White House through the basement. According to my orders I followed him, and was alone with President Lincoln for the first time.

We crossed the garden, which lay to the west, where the executive offices are now. Mr. Lincoln was bent on his nightly visit to Secretary Stanton at the War Department. I stole a glance up at him, at the homely face rising so far above me. The strength of it is not lessened in my memory by what would seem to me now a grotesque setting of rough shawl and silk hat. He looked to me just like his picture, but gentler. I will confess that I was nervous when I accompanied him that first time. I hope it was not from any fear for myself. I seemed to realize suddenly that there was only myself between this man and possible danger. The feeling wore off in time, though it was apt to come back at any moment of special responsibility, as, for instance, on the entrance into Richmond—but I mustn't get ahead of my story.

That night, as I said, I was a little nervous. The President noticed it. He seemed to know how I felt, too. I had fallen into line behind him, but he motioned me to walk by his side. He began to talk to me in a kindly way, as though I were a bashful boy whom he wanted to put at his ease, instead of a man appointed to guard him. In part, of course, his motive must have been the dislike of seeming to be guarded, of which I have spoken. But his manner was due to the intuitive sympathy with every one, of which I afterward saw so many instances. It was shown particularly toward those who were subordinate to him. The statesmen who came to consult him, those who had it in their power to influence the policy of the party which had chosen him, never had the consideration from Mr. Lincoln that he gave the humblest of those who served him.

A few strides of the President's long legs—a few more of mine—brought us to the old-fashioned turnstile that divided the White House grounds from the enclosure of the War Department. Mr. Lincoln talked, in his slow, soft voice, chiefly about the reception through which he had just gone.

"I am glad it is over," he said.

I ventured to ask if he was tired.

"Yes, it does tire me to shake hands with so many people," he answered. "Especially now when there is so much other work to do. And most of the guests come out of mere curiosity."

With these words and the half-sigh which followed we entered the east door of the War Department. In those days that was a small, mean, two-story building, just in front of the Navy Department. We went immediately to Mr. Stanton's office, which was on the second floor, on the north front, and overlooked Pennsylvania Avenue and the White House. There,

2

at the door, I waited for him until his conference with Secretary Stanton was over. Then I accompanied him back to the White House. From the moment Mr. Lincoln spoke to me so kindly I felt at home in my new duties. I never lost the feeling which came then that, while the President was so great, he was my friend. The White House never awed me again.

For the next three weeks, while I was on duty the first half of the night, I went to the War Department with Mr. Lincoln every evening. He usually talked to me. Several times the topic was the one my presence naturally suggested—the possibility of an attempt being made on his life. Later on I will speak of this more in detail. One time while he was talking he reached out and took my hand, and I walked on for a few paces with my hand in his warm, kind grasp. We always took the same route, because there was less chance of being observed than if we went by the big north entrance. There was then no telegraph station in the White House, so the President had to go to Secretary Stanton's oflQce to get the latest news from the front. Since there was practical advantage in going himself, for he could be more free from interruption there when he remained to discuss matters of policy (if the news of the night necessitated any action), it would never have occurred to Mr. Lincoln to regard his own personal dignity and wait for his Secretary to come to him. I had opportunity to observe the difference in the attitude of Secretary Stanton's employees from ours toward the President.

The great War Secretary was a martinet for discipline, and none of the clerks wanted to be around when there was bad news from the front. He always seemed to me a very bitter, cruel man. Still, there is no doubt that he was a great man. His own subordinates, though they might be afraid of his irascible temper, admired him and were loyal.

Beginning with the 1st of February, I was on duty the second half of the night, from twelve to eight in the morning. Often I had to wait for the President to return from the War Department; even when he came back comparatively early it was midnight before he got to bed. His bedroom was a small chamber in the southwest corner of the house. Mrs. Lincoln's was a larger room adjoining it. Mr. Lincoln always said, "Good-night, Crook," when he passed me on his way to his room, but gave no instructions for my guidance. He was not interrupted after he retired unless there were important telegrams. Even when awakened suddenly from a deep sleep—which is the most searching test of one's temper that I know—he was never ruffled, but received the message and the messenger kindly. No employee of the White House ever saw the President moved beyond his usual controlled calm. When the first of these interruptions occurred and I had to enter the President's room, I looked around me with a good deal of interest. The place the President slept in was a noteworthy spot to me. It was handsomely furnished; the bedstead, bureau, and wash-stand were of heavy mahogany, the bureau and wash-stand with marble tops; the chairs were of rosewood. Like all the other chambers, it was covered with a carpet.

All night I walked up and down the long corridor which, running east and west, divided the second story of the White House in half. Usually the household, with the exception of Mr. Lincoln, was asleep when I began my watch. Occasionally, however, something kept them up, and I saw them go to their rooms. I learned very soon who slept behind each door that I passed in my patrol. Somehow one feels acquainted with people when one is the only one, besides the doorkeeper, awake in a great house, and is responsible for the safety of them all. As I said before, the corridor divided the private apartments of the White House into two long rows, one facing south, the other north. Beginning at the west, on the south side, was the President's room, Mrs. Lincoln's just east of it and communicating. Then followed a guest-room, which communicated with Mrs. Lincoln's. Next to this was the library, just over the Blue Room, and, like it, an octagon in shape; this was used as the family sitting-room. In Mr. Lincoln's time a private passage-way ran through the reception room adjoining the library to the President's office beyond. By this the President could have access during his long working-day to his own apartments without being seen by the strangers who always filled the reception-room. The small room in the southeast comer was the office of Mr. Lincoln's secretaries—Mr. Hay and Mr. Nicolay. On the other side of the corridor Mr. Nicolay, when he slept in the White House, had the chamber at the eastern end. Next to his was the state guest-room, which, unlike any other room in the house, possessed a large four-poster bed with a tester and rich canopy. Between this and Taddie's room—Taddie was the only child at the White House at this time — three smaller rooms and a bath-room intervened. The boy was just opposite his father.

When in my patrol I came near to the door of the President's room I could hear his deep breathing. Sometimes, after a day of unusual anxiety, I have heard him moan in his sleep. It gave me a curious sensation. While the expression of Mr. Lincoln's face was always sad when he was quiet, it gave one the assurance of calm. He never seemed to doubt the wisdom of an action when he had once decided on it. And so when he was in a way defenceless in his sleep it made me feel the pity that would have been almost an impertinence when he was awake. I would stand there and listen until a sort of panic stole over me. If he felt the weight of things so heavily, how much worse the situation of the country must be than any of us realized! At last I would walk softly away, feeling as if I had been listening at a keyhole.

II

THE WHITE HOUSE FAMILY AND OTHER PEOPLE

ON the 15th of February I went on day duty. During that time I necessarily saw more of the every-day Hfe of the President and his family. Everything was much simpler than it is now. More of the family life was open to the scrutiny of the people about. I remember very well one incident which would have been impossible at any time since. I was sent for by the President, who was in his own room. In response to my knock he called out: "Come in!" I entered. To my great surprise I saw that he was struggling with a needle and thread. He was sewing a button on his trousers. "All right," he said, looking at me with a twinkle in his eye. "Just wait until I repair damages."

Mr. Lincoln, as I saw him every morning, in the carpet slippers he wore in the house and the black clothes no tailor could make really fit his gaunt, bony frame, was a homely enough figure. The routine of his life was simple, too; it would have seemed a treadmill to most of us. He was an early riser; when I came on duty, at eight in the morning, he was often already dressed and reading in the library. There was a big table near the centre of the room; there I

THE WHITE HOUSE FAMILY

have seen him reading many times. And the book? We have all heard of the President's fondness for Shakespeare, how he infuriated Secretary Stanton by reading Hamlet while they were waiting for returns from Gettysburg; we know, too, how he kept cabinet meetings waiting while he read them the latest of Petroleum V. Nasby's witticisms. But it was the Bible which I saw him reading while most of the household still slept.

Mr. and Mrs. Lincoln breakfasted at nine. Mr. Lincoln was a hearty eater. He never lost his taste for the things a growing farmer's boy would like. He was particularly fond of bacon. Plentiful and wholesome food was one of the means by which he kept up his strength, which was taxed almost beyond endurance in those days. Even hostile newspapers commented angrily on the strain to which the President was subjected, and prophesied that he would collapse unless some of the pressure of business was removed. But in spite of his gauntness he was a man of great physical endurance. Every inch of his six feet four inches was seasoned and tempered force.

He needed all of it; for from half-past nine, when he came into his office, until midnight, when he went to bed, his work went on, almost without cessation. He had very little outdoor life. An occasional drive with Mrs. Lincoln in the afternoon, a more occasional horseback ride, a few moments to fill his lungs with outside air while he walked the few paces to the War Department, was the sum of it. Mrs. Lincoln was anxious that he should have some recreation. I have carried messages to him for her when he was lingering in his office, held by some business. One beautiful afternoon she sent for him so many times that she became impatient, and told me to tell him that he must come. He got up with an expression of great submission and said :

"I guess I would better go."

The friends who were with him teased him a little about Mrs. Lincoln's show of authority.

"If you knew how little harm it does me," he said, "and how much good it does her, you wouldn't wonder that I am meek." And he went out laughing.

The White House and its surroundings during wartime had much the appearance of a Southern plantation— straggling and easy-going. On the east side of the house beyond the extension—since removed— which corresponded to the conservatory on the west, was a row of outhouses, a carriage-house and a woodshed among them. Back and east were the kitchen-garden and the stable where the President's two horses were kept. South of the house was a short stretch of lawn bounded by a high iron fence. Still beyond was rough undergrowth and marsh to the river. North and to the west was a garden, divided from the rest of the grounds by tall fences. It was a real country garden, with peach-trees and strawberry-vines as well as flowers. It was winter, of course, when I was there, but the people about the house told me that Mrs. Lincoln used to pick the strawberries for the table herself.

I saw a good deal of Mrs. Lincoln while I was on

day duty. Very few who were not about the house realized how exacting were the duties of her position. She was, of course, much absorbed by social duties, which presented difficulties no other President's wife has had to contend against. The house was filled, the receptions were crowded, with all sorts of people, of all varieties of political conviction, who felt, according to the temper of the time, that they had a perfect right to take up the President's time with their discourse and to demand of Mrs. Lincoln social consideration. Nor could there be discrimination used at the state dinner-parties; any man who was bearing a part in the events of the day must be invited—and his women folks. Jim Lane, rough old Kansas fighter, dined beside Salmon P. Chase with his patrician instincts. The White House has never, during my forty years' service, been so entirely given over to the public as during Mr. Lincoln's administration. The times were too anxious to make of social affairs anything more than an aid to more serious matters. It was necessary, of course; but it made it difficult for a first-lady-in-the-land with any preferences or prejudices not to make enemies on every hand.

Mrs. Lincoln had to give some time to household affairs. Everything was comparatively simple at that time; there were fewer servants than have been considered necessary since. The first duty of Mrs. Lincoln's day was a consultation with the steward, whose name was Stack-pole. The cook was an old-time negro woman. A good deal of domestic supervision was necessary with the mistress of the house.

For state dinners the regular staff was entirely inadequate; a French caterer was called in, who furnished everything, including waiters. It fell to Mrs. Lincoln to choose the set of china which the White House needed at this stage. It was, in my opinion, the handsomest that has ever been used there. In the centre was an eagle surrounded by clouds; the rim was a solid band of maroon. The coloring was soft and pretty, and the design patriotic. The President's wife found time, too, to investigate cases of need that were brought to her attention, and to help. I know of such cases. She was kind to all the employees of the White House. I think she was very generally liked.

Robert Lincoln was an officer on General Grant's staff, and was in Washington only at inauguration time and for a few days at the time of his father's death. But he was a manly, genial young fellow, and we all liked him. Taddie—he was christened Thomas—was the pet of the whole household. He was ten years old at the time. I wish I could show what a capital little fellow he was. I think I will have to take a few minutes to talk of Taddie.

Since the death of the older boy, Willie, which almost broke his father's heart, Mr. Lincoln had kept Tad with him almost constantly. When he had a few minutes to spare he would make a child of himself to play with the boy. We all liked to see the President romp up and down the corridors with Tad, playing horse, turn and turn about, or blind-man's buff. Mr. Lincoln was such a sad-looking man usual

THE WHITE HOUSE FAMILY

ly, it seemed good to have him happy. And he was happy when he was playing with the boy. I am sure the times when he was really resting were when he was galloping around with Tad on his great shoulders. And when the President was too busy to play with him, Tad would play quietly, near as he could get, making a man of himself to be company to his father. That was the sort of a little fellow he was.

He was a tender-hearted boy. Of course, all sorts of people found it out and tried to get at the President through him. Mr. Lincoln was criticised sometimes for being too lenient when the boy begged for some one he had been asked to help. But I don't believe mercy was a bad thing to be overdone in those days. Tad's loving heart was like in kind to the one that made the President suffer so when he had to be severe. The boy was like his father; he looked like him. But with Tad there was no realization of anything else to confuse him. And when Mr. Lincoln was what some people called too indulgent he was just listening to what I believe was the greatest thing in him—his great human heart. And I don't believe that anything but good ever came of it, either.

I remember one poor woman who came to the White House to get her husband out of prison. She found Taddie in the corridor, and told him that her boys and girls were cold and starving because their father was shut up and couldn't work for them. Poor little Taddie couldn't wait a minute. He ran to his father and begged him to have the man set free. The President was busy with some important papers, and told him, rather absent-mindedly, that he would look into the case as soon as he had time. But Tad was thinking of the woman, and he clung to his father's knees and begged until the President had to listen, and, listening, became interested. So, after all. Taddie could run back to tell the woman that her husband would be set at liberty. I wish you could have seen the child's face. The woman blessed him and cried, and Taddie cried, and I am not sure that my own eyes were above suspicion.

Tad had a great many friends among the men who were about the White House in various capacities. I myself have a letter from him written from Chicago in July, 1865, a few months after the family had left the White House. It was written for Tad by Mrs. Lincoln, and the business part of it—I had asked if there would be a good opening for me in Chicago— was her own, of course. But the rest is all Taddie:

Near Chicago, *July*, 1865.

My dear Friend,—I received your letter two weeks since, and circumstances prevented an earlier reply. If you come out to Chicago, I expect you can do as well here as anywhere else. We will be very glad to have you live here, for I consider you one of my best friends. You could get a pass, perhaps, from the War Department, and come out here and have a try at least. Your board would not cost you more than in Washington—you will know best about it. A gentleman who does business in the city wants a clerk; he lives out here and goes in every day. He says he must write a good hand and not be very slow. Tell us how Charlie is coming on, and Dana Pendel—none of them ever write. Tell us about the new people in the house. All news will interest us.

Your friend truly,

TADDIE.

THE WHITE HOUSE FAMILY

"Charlie" was Charles Forbes, an Irishman. He was the footman, and one of Tad's friends. "Dana" Pendel was Thomas Pendel, the doorkeeper, of whom Taddie was also very fond.

James Haliday was another friend. He was a carpenter who worked about the place, and was directed by the President to put up a stage and arrange things for theatrical performances in the little room just over the entrance. That was when Tad was stage-struck and found it necessary to endow a theatre of his own. Perry Kelly—a boy of about Tad's age, whose father was a tinner on Pennsylvania Avenue between Seventeenth and Eighteenth Streets—was the only other actor, and the audience was composed chiefly of any employees of the place who could be coerced.

Haliday, who is living now in Boston, was also a member of Tad's military company. Like all other boys of those exciting times. Tad had the military fever. But he was allowed to gratify it in a way not open to other boys. The Secretary of War gave him a lieutenant's commission and an order on the arsenal for twenty-five guns; a pretty uniform was made for him. The guns were kept in the basement in a room opening off of the furnace-room, and the Lieutenant had his headquarters in a little place opposite the laundry. He not only drilled his company outside and marched them through the house, but he kept them on guard duty at night to relieve the "bucktails," as the military guard of the White House was familiarly called. The first night of this military despotism Haliday, who had been appointed a sergeant, appeared before his superior. He saluted and said:

"Mr. Lieutenant, I would like to have a pass this evening." The lieutenant acknowledged the salute and replied:

"All right; I will give the sergeant a pass." He scribbled something on a piece of paper and handed it to him. The other members of the company were kept up until ten o'clock that night on guard duty. The next day Haliday, knowing what he had escaped, again sought Lieutenant Tad in his basement headquarters. Taking off his hat, he asked for a pass. But the lieutenant "got mad."

"What kind of a soldier are you? You want a pass every evening!" he said.

"All right, Mr. Lieutenant." Haliday was meek enough now. "I will be on duty to-night."

In about an hour Tad sent his sergeant to the National Theatre and left word with another underling that when Haliday returned he was to be given his pass, after all. That night the rest of the company was kept on duty until one o'clock. But that was somewhat too strenuous. Either there was mutiny or the commander-in-chief interfered, for that was the last night they were on duty outside.

Tad's taste of command in military matters was so pleasing that he began to enlarge his field of operations. Haliday, aided by the gardener, was about to take up the carpet in the congressional, or state, dining-room. The long table made it some-

THE WHITE HOUSE FAMILY

what difficult, and they were debating about which end to attack it from, when Tad appeared. He surveyed the field.

"Jim," he said to Haliday, "I have a favor to ask of you. Jim, grant it," he coaxed.

Jim, of course, said "Yes," as every one had a way of doing—and yet it wasn't because it was the President's son.

"Now, Jim," he said, taking an attitude of command, "you work with the other man. I will boss the job." And Haliday, talking about it, asserts to this day: "He told us just how to go about it. And there was no one could engineer it better than he did." Haliday tells, too, that Tad often borrowed money of him when some poor man asked him for help and the boy had nothing in his pockets. "And he always paid me back. He never forgot it."

Taddie could never speak very plainly. He had his own language; the names that he gave some of us we like to remember to-day. The President was "papa-day," which meant "papa dear." Tom Pendel was "Tom Pen," and I was "Took." But for all his baby tongue he had a man's heart, and in some things a man's mind. I believe he was the best companion Mr. Lincoln ever had—one who always understood him, and whom he always understood.

After I had had time enough to become somewhat used to seeing the White House family every day, the crowd of men and women who filled the anteroom to the President's office began to interest me. There were all sorts of people—mothers who wanted to have their husbands returned to them from the army, wounded soldiers who wanted help, ambitious young men who wanted positions, self-appointed advisers who wanted to be listened to, and sisters of deserters who wanted reprieves. The office-seekers were the most persistent and unreasonable. An experience that a friend of mine—Mr. F. J. Whipple, of New York—had with the President will show how Mr. Lincoln felt about them.

Mr. Whipple called at the White House one day. As he was a little early, he had to wait in the hall opposite the President's office. He had not been there long when Mr. Lincoln came in from the private part of the house. Whipple rose, saying:

"This is Mr. Lincoln, I believe."

"Yes. What can I do for you?"

"Nothing, sir. You have not an office I would accept."

Mr. Lincoln slapped him on the shoulder.

"Is it possible! Come into my office. I want to look at you. It is a curiosity to see a man who does not want an office. You might as well try to dip the Potomac dry as to satisfy them all."

They had a few minutes' more conversation, while the President idly made some lines on a paper. A few days later I was in the room with the President when a prominent senator called upon him. Seeing a pencil-sketch on the desk, the visitor asked what it was.

"It is the portrait of the one man who does not want an office," Mr. Lincoln replied.

THE WHITE HOUSE FAMILY

On one occasion the President was going over, with Secretary Stanton, some applications for commissions in the army when they came to the last one on the list.

"This fellow hasn't any endorser," said the President. Then he glanced at the letter—became interested. "It's a good, straightforward letter," he said. "I'll be his endorser." And the young man had his lieutenancy."

One thing which gives me happiness to remember happened on the 2d of March. I was drafted, and the other guards with me. Frankly, I didn't want to go. I had served in the army already; I had a young wife and a young son at home to hold me. I couldn't afford to pay for a substitute. So I joined the ranks of the people with grievances whom for some time I had been watching and went to the President. I found him in his own room, in dressing-gown and slippers. I told him that I had been drafted, and asked him if he could do anything in my case and in that of Alexander Smith, who was my special friend on the force. He listened to my story as patiently as if he had not heard hundreds like it. I like to remember how kindly he looked at me. When I had finished, he said:

"Well, I can't spare you. Come into my office."

I followed him as a child would follow his father. He seated himself at the desk and wrote on a small card a note to Provost-Marshal Frye and told me to take it to him and get the answer. Years after this the Hon. Robert T. Lincoln gave me the card when he was Secretary of War, and I have it still. It reads:

These two of my men, Crook and Alexander, are drafted, and I cannot spare them. P. M. G., please fix.

March 2, 1865.   A. Lincoln.

"Alexander" was Alexander Smith, whose last name the President forgot. The other men had their cases "fixed" through Mrs. Lincoln.

It is something to have in President Lincoln's own hand—even though the motive was largely kindness on his own part—the assurance that he couldn't spare me.

Naturally enough the events of the time which are most vivid to me are ones, like this, in which I took some part. Of other things I often have only the recollection that any one else in Washington would have had. Of the ceremonies when the President was a second time installed in office, for instance, I remember very little, or of the inaugural ball—for I wasn't on duty at either of those events. There were the usual exercises, of course, at the inauguration and the ball in the Patent Office. We were all interested in that because it was rumored that Robert Lincoln, who was popular with us, escorted the daughter of Senator Harlan, to whom he was afterward married. Of the great public reception at the White House the evening of the 5th I remember chiefly the havoc it wrought. The White House looked as if a regiment of rebel troops had been quartered there—with permission to forage. The crowds were enormous, and there were some rough people present. A fever of vandalism seemed to seize them. We had always found that some odds and ends had been carried away as souvenirs after public reception, but the damage created by this one was something monstrous. I suppose if it had not been that the President was assassinated so soon afterward I wouldn't remember it so vividly. But looking back, it seems some premonition that there would not be much more of Mr. Lincoln's administration must have come to them and made them lawless. They wanted to get mementos while they could. A great piece of red brocade, a yard square almost, was cut from the window-hangings of the East Room, and another piece, not quite so large, from a curtain in the Green Room. Besides this, flowers from the floral design in the lace curtains were cut out, evidently for an ornament for the top of pincushions or something of the sort. Some arrests were made, after the reception, of persons concerned in the disgraceful business.

These things distressed the President greatly. I can hardly understand why, when he was so calm about things usually, these acts of rowdyism should have impressed him so painfully. It was the senseless violence of it that puzzled him.

"Why should they do it?" he said to me. "How can they?"

But Secretary McCulloch's appointment to succeed Mr. Chase as Secretary of the Treasury seems to me about the biggest event of the period—for I really notified him. It happened this way: Before the

President had given Mr. McCulloch any indication that he intended to appoint him, he sent me over to the Treasury, where McCulloch was Comptroller of the Currency. I was to ask "Secretary McCulloch" if he would please come to the President. Whether it was just absent-mindedness in Mr. Lincoln or whether is was just his own way of doing things I don't know. But I went over and repeated the message just as he gave it. Mr. McCulloch blushed like a girl.

" I am not the Secretary," he said. "There is some mistake."

"You will be as soon as you see the President, then," I replied. He went over with me then without further protest. Years after I had a letter from Mr. McCulloch alluding to the incident and to the way the President looked when he told him he wished to appoint him to the position Secretary Chase had left vacant.

Late in March Thaddeus Stevens, of Pennsylvania, called upon Mr. Lincoln to urge "a more vigorous prosecution of the war," which was the watchword of those men of his own party who criticised the President. Mr. Stevens was one of the ablest, as well as one of the most radical men then in Congress, but he was a very impatient man. The President listened patiently to Mr. Stevens's argument, and when he had concluded he looked at his visitor a moment in silence. Then he said, looking at Mr. Stevens very shrewdly:

"Stevens, this is a pretty big hog we are trying to

catch, and to hold when we do catch him. We must take care that he doesn't slip away from us." Mr. Stevens had to be satisfied with the answer.

A general kindliness marked the President's manner toward all who came to see him. The greater part of the callers were there for one occasion only. With others we grew familiar. General Sheridan was a conspicuous figure. He was a short man with enormous and disproportionate width of shoulder and chest. He had a broad red face, and wore a little mustache and imperial. Dr. Gurley, the pastor of the New York Avenue Presbyterian Church, which the President attended, was often there, as was Surgeon Barnes, the White House physician. Mr. Lincoln admired General Halleck and had great belief in him; his manner, in its cordiality, showed it. General Farnsworth, too, was a special friend of the President's. Speed, the Attorney-General, was Mr. Lincoln's oldest friend in Washington; there were friendship and confidence between the two men. Marshal Ward Lamon, who had been Mr. Lincoln's law partner, was a warm and anxious friend, always most solicitous for the President's safety. Secretary Welles, who was an impressive and handsome old man, with his great stature and bushy white hair, the President especially liked.

In General Grant he had the most unbounded confidence. The two men understood each other. There never was a less assuming man than the General. I remember seeing him in the corridor at one of the evening receptions just before he entered. He had on a shabby army overcoat and a slouch-hat. I couldn't help contrasting both his appearance and ability with that of other magnificent gold-laced officers within. I have often seen the President and General Grant poring over maps together. I know that no move was made by his general that the President did not understand and approve. And when, later on, they met at Petersburg, when it was evident that Mr. Lincoln's faith in Grant was to be realized, he was positively affectionate. He looked as if, instead of merely shaking hands, he would have liked to hug the General.

The thing that most impressed me was that, with one exception, Mr. Lincoln was not influenced in his judgment of men in the slightest degree either by personal liking or by enmity. It was the more remarkable in a man so well fitted for warm friendship, so lovable. At this time of grave personal danger his only standard of measurement was fitness to serve the Government. Men came in a never-ending stream to the White House. While, as I have said, his constant attitude was one of kindly consideration, it was also one of control. He was eager to recognize the ability and character of men who were his bitter political enemies; he allowed his personal friend to retire to private life if he knew that the general interest would be promoted by so doing.

To the men who criticised him, as did Thaddeus Stevens, he showed no impatience; to the men who insulted him, as did Duff Green, he answered nothing; to Salmon P. Chase, whose vanity made him disloyal, in spite of high character and great attainments, he was patience itself. In connection with the appointment of Chase to the Chief-Justiceship there is a good story which, I believe, has never been told. It was given to me by Mr. John B. Alley, who was Congressman from Massachusetts.

It was generally known that Mr. Chase wanted to be nominated for the Presidency by the convention which chose Lincoln for his second term. Mr. Chase consulted Sumner, Alley, and other friends on the subject, and they dissuaded him, urging him instead to seek the Chief-Justiceship, for which he had peculiar qualifications. Chase at first turned a deaf ear to their entreaties, but before leaving for his home in Ohio he said he would think the matter over. For several weeks Mr. Alley heard nothing of him. At the end of that time the Massachusetts Congressman received a letter from Mr. Chase, saying that if the appointment were tendered him he would accept.

Mr. Alley immediately saw Mr. Lincoln and put the case before him in the strongest possible light. The President listened very patiently until he had finished. Then he began to talk. He gave reasons for not appointing Mr. Chase. He spoke of Mr. Chase's dislike of the President. He talked feelingly of the many hard things Mrs. Sprague, Mr. Chase's daughter, had said of the President. All of this left on Mr. Alley the impression that it was useless to press the matter further.

He went to his home greatly disappointed. Very early the next morning a messenger came from the

White House asking him to call at his earliest convenience. He went immediately to the White House. Mr. Lincoln met him very cordially, but with his own twinkle in his eye.

"Alley," he said, "I just want to tell you that I am going to send Chase's nomination to the Senate today. He is to be Chief Justice of the United States." Alley was so astonished that he could not speak for a moment. Then he said:

"Mr. President, I am very glad to know it, but—from what you said—I thought the case was hopeless." "Oh," replied Mr. Lincoln, "I only wanted to show you what could be said on the other side. I ought not to blame Chase for the things his daughter said about me."

The peculiar humor of the situation was not apparent to Mr. Alley at the time. The idea of making Chase Chief Justice is known now to have originated with Mr. Lincoln himself, and had been fully determined before Mr. Alley made his plea. One can imagine the President's inward appreciation of his own little joke while he urged with all seriousness that the position he was fitted for should be withheld from Salmon P. Chase because the daughter had said feminine things—possibly about the President's social demeanor.

Earlier than this the resignation of Montgomery Blair from the position of Postmaster-General showed a like absence of personal feeling in Mr. Lincoln's public policy. Mr. Blair was a personal friend of the President, who had the warmest possible feeling for

ABRAHAM LINCOLN

THE WHITE HOUSE FAMILY

him and a conviction of his ability and integrity. But Mr. Blair grew out of sympathy with some members of his party, and his usefulness was impaired by frequent disputes with leading Republicans. Whatever Mr. Lincoln's opinion was as to the relative right or wrong of the disputants, he realized, as did Mr. Blair himself, that the party must be united in its policy. Therefore he allowed Mr. Blair to resign, much as personally he had wished him to remain.

The President's relationship to Secretary Stanton was another instance of Mr. Lincoln's marvellous self-control. Where the good of the nation was involved he didn't even see things that related to himself alone. Secretary Stanton was a strong man and devoted to his country. I believe, too, that he really loved the President. But while he recognized Mr. Lincoln's greatness and was loyal, those traits of Mr. Lincoln's which were antipathetic to his own character irritated him sometimes almost beyond endurance. Mr. Stanton was not a man of much self-control. The President's tenderness of heart seemed to him weakness. The fondness for reading and for jesting, which every day restored the balance in the President's over-weighted mind, seemed to Mr. Stanton something approaching imbecility. He was furious once when Mr. Lincoln delayed a cabinet meeting to read the witticisms of Petroleum V. Nasby. When the President, during hours of anxious waiting for news from a great battle, was apparently absorbed in Hamlet, Mr. Stanton, whose invectives were varied, called him, I have heard, "a baboon."

To such expressions of a natural impatience Mr. Lincoln opposed a placid front. More than that, he was placid. He knew Secretary Stanton's intense, irritable nature. He knew how the excitement of the time tried men's tempers and shattered their nerves. He himself, apparently, was the only one who was not to be allowed the indulgence of giving way. So Mr. Stanton's indignation passed unnoticed. The two men were often at variance when it came to matters of discipline in the army. On one occasion, I have heard. Secretary Stanton was particularly angry with one of the generals. He was eloquent about him. "I would like to tell him what I think of him!" he stormed.

"Why don't you?" Mr. Lincoln agreed. "Write it all down—do."

Mr. Stanton wrote his letter. When it was finished he took it to the President. The President listened to it all.

"All right. Capital!" he nodded. "And now, Stanton, what are you going to do with it?"

"Do with it? Why, send it, of course!"

"I wouldn't," said the President. "Throw it in the waste-paper basket."

"But it took me two days to write—"

"Yes, yes, and it did you ever so much good. You feel better now. That is all that is necessary. Just throw it in the basket."

After a little more expostulation, into the basket it went.

I have spoken of an exception to the rule of the

President's freedom from personal feeling in his relations to the public men of the time. That exception was Charles Sumner. It is a curious fact that a man who was one of the leaders in the party which had twice chosen Mr. Lincoln to be President, who was an exponent of the belief which determined the most momentous action of Mr. Lincoln's career—the emancipation of the slaves—should have been the only man, so far as my knowledge goes, to obtain the President's dislike.

The reason of this dislike may never be satisfactorily determined. With another man than Mr. Lincoln the explanation would have been a perfectly simple one. Most people know that Sumner was often the President's severe critic. He besieged Mr. Lincoln with advice in and out of season. Few of the President's public utterances, according to Senator Sumner, were free from grave faults—his condemnation included both principles expressed and manner of expression. All of this Mr. Lincoln accepted patiently and humorously, as was his custom, passing over the tediousness of it all because of the high character and attainments of the man. Not so many persons know, possibly, that Sumner was actually in opposition to Mr. Lincoln. Just before the President's second nomination Senator Sumner was involved, with Greeley, Godwin, and others, in a movement against Mr. Lincoln. That again, if the President ever knew of Sumner's defection, he might have passed over as magnanimously as he did the opposetion of Chase. It is doubtful that he did know of it;

when these men found that their movement was hopeless they fell into line and helped to elect Mr. Lincoln.

Senator Sumner was a fine-looking man. His presence was tall and commanding; he was well-groomed, even exquisite in his appointments. He affected the English type in his clothes, wearing large checks and plaids, and was fond of displaying white spats—which were not, at that time, often seen upon our statesmen.

Mr. Sumner was a friend of the Chases, a particularly warm friend of Mrs. Kate Chase Sprague, who sympathized with him in his matrimonial difficulties. He was also a friend of Mrs. Lincoln. Not only was he present at state receptions and dinners (which, of course, would argue nothing), but he was Mrs. Lincoln's escort at the second inaugural ball—especially invited, he told a friend, by Mr. Lincoln; and he was a member, with Senator and Mrs. Harlan, the future father and mother in law of Robert T. Lincoln, of the gay party which Mrs. Lincoln brought down to City Point after the fall of Richmond. The President did not interfere with Mrs. Lincoln's social relations. This is only one instance of Mr. Lincoln's largeness of mind, which did not allow personal matters to influence his judgment.

This was particularly noteworthy in the case of Sumner because, added to the fact that the Senator antagonized him in public matters, was the personal dislike of which I spoke. If what Elphonso Dunn told me was true, this was great enough to cause Mr. Lincoln to give instructions, on one occasion, that Senator Sumner should not be admitted to the White House. Dunn was on duty in the corridor, and the matter naturally made a great impression on him.

III

THE ENTRANCE INTO RICHMOND

ABOUT noon of March 23d the President called me into his room, and said:

"Crook, I want you to accompany me to City Point, Virginia. We leave this afternoon. If you have any preparations to make, you must attend to them at once." I hurried home to get the few necessary clothes and say good-bye to my family. It was late in the afternoon when I rejoined Mr. Lincoln on board the River Queen, which was lying at the Seventh Street wharf.

There were a good many people on the quay watching the boat. Rumors of the President's departure were about—I'm sure I don't know how; there had been no announcement—and everybody wanted to know where he was going. It took very little to get up an alarm during those last months of the war. But the questions were not answered, and the crowd had to content itself with a glimpse of the President on the deck. They watched while the River Queen left her moorings and slowly steamed down the Potomac.

The President was accompanied by Mrs. Lincoln, Taddie, Captain Penrose of the army, and myself.

THE ENTRANCE INTO RICHMOND

Penrose had been detailed to have general charge of the party. He was a tall, fine-looking man, fair like an Englishman. Bradford, who was the captain of the River Queen, had done everything he could on such short notice to make his guests comfortable. He took me all over the boat and showed me, with some pride, how he had had the state-rooms fitted up. Taddie's investigating mind led him everywhere. Before he went to bed he had studied every screw of the engine and he knew and counted among his friends every man of the crew. They all liked him, too.

Mr. Lincoln watched the city until he could see it no more. At first he was interested in the sights along the shores. But as we drew near Alexandria he turned back to catch a last glimpse of the city. All the sadness of his face came out now when he was quiet. I realized, as I had never done before, what the war meant to him and how anxious he was. It was growing dark, and the air was raw and chilly. But he stayed on deck until we had passed Alexandria. Then every one went inside.

Captain Bradford's long experience of the Potomac had made him acquainted with the histories of spies and blockade-runners who, in the early days of the war, had stolen across the river to the Maryland side. He told us many exciting incidents; he pointed out the landings they had made. The President was very much interested, and kept the captain busy answering questions. It was nearly midnight when he went to bed.

Tad and I had a state - room together. Toward morning I was startled out of a sound sleep by some one entering the room. Before I could speak I heard Mrs. Lincoln's voice: "It is I, Crook. It is growing colder, and I came in to see if my little boy has covers enough on him." In a little while I was awakened again. This time it was by a sensation of great discomfort. I will have to explain that I was a countryman and had been no great traveller. I had never slept on a boat before. It appeared to me that the steamer was slowly climbing up one side of a hill and then rushing down the other. I have since learned that I was seasick. I know I felt awfully blue. Taddie was still asleep. I dressed as best I could, and hurried out to demand from the captain what was the matter with the boat. He laughed at me a little, and then informed me that we were in Chesapeake Bay, nearing Fortress Monroe, and that it was a little rough.

Evidently Mr. Lincoln was a better sailor than I was, for he came on deck in a few minutes looking very much rested.

"I'm feeling splendidly," he said. "Is breakfast ready?" He did full justice to the delicious fish when it was served. When we steamed into the mouth of the James and calmer water I recovered my spirits and found that I was hungry.

It was after dark on the 24th when we reached City Point. It was a beautiful sight at this time, with the many-colored lights of the boats in the harbor and the lights of the town straggling up the high

THE ENTRANCE INTO RICHMOND

bluffs of the shore, crowned by the lights from Grant's headquarters at the top.

It was known at Grant headquarters that the President was coming, and a lookout had been kept. As soon as the River Queen was made fast to the wharf. General Grant with some members of his staff came aboard. They had a long consultation with the President, at the end of which Mr. Lincoln appeared particularly happy. General Grant had evidently made him feel that the end of the conflict was at hand, nearer than he had expected. After General Grant had gone, Taddie and I went ashore to take a look at the place by starlight. We did not get many steps from the steamer before we were halted by a sentinel. I explained who we were, but Taddie thought he would go back. He said he did not like the looks of things. He wasn't used to being halted by sentinels who didn't know who he was. We went back to the boat. Everybody was up until late. The President and Mrs. Lincoln talked of the trip; they were in very good spirits.

The next day, the 25th, was clear and warmer. We had an opportunity of seeing one of the great centres of the war. In Mr. Lincoln's estimation it was the critical point, and he had placed his lieutenant-general, the man in whom he had most faith, in charge. The Appomattox and the James come together at City Point. The harbor thus made is overhung with high bluffs. On the top of one bluff was a group of houses, which Grant and his staff used as headquarters. The harbor was crowded with craft of all kinds—fishing-boats, row-boats, sail-boats, transports, and passenger-boats. From higher ground in the vicinity could be seen the tents of Lee's army. It was a busy camp, and everything was in motion. Just west of our troops was the long, curved line of Lee's intrenchments, stretching from Petersburg, south of the James and fifteen miles from City Point, to Richmond, northwest of City Point and nearly double that distance.

We all went ashore and visited General Grant's headquarters. After the greetings, General Grant invited the President to take a ride to the front, where General Meade was in command. When we started, Mr. Lincoln was seen to be on a black pony belonging to General Grant. The name of the animal was Jeff Davis. Everybody laughed at the idea, and at the sight, too, for the President's feet nearly touched the ground. Mr. Lincoln was a good horseman, but always rather an ungainly sight on horseback. He laughed at himself this time, and said, "Well, he may be Jeff Davis and a little too small for me, but he is a good horse."

Mrs. Lincoln rode in an army ambulance with Mrs. Grant, who was a member of the party for that day.

It had been intended when we started for City Point that there should be a grand review of the troops. But the Confederates were active the first part of the ten days before we left to visit Richmond, and the preparations for the final operations before Petersburg were being made the latter part of the time. There was a lull in between, but never a time

THE ENTRANCE INTO RICHMOND

when it was possible to draw all the soldiers away from their positions. So we never had the grand review.

We saw some lively skirmishing, however, between the picket-lines of the two forces while we were at General Meade's headquarters. We were on a hill just east of where the troops were engaged; it was not more than a quarter of a mile away from the wood where the fighting was in progress. We could see the shells as they were fired; but while we were there they burst in the air and did no damage. The President asked whether the position was not too close for the comfort of his party. When he was assured that there was no danger, he remained two hours watching the struggle, and turned away only when the firing ceased.

On the 26th Mr. Lincoln visited General Ord's command on the northern bank of the James and reviewed the troops. They were brought out in dress parade, and went through the evolutions of actual war. Mrs. Ord was a member of the party. To get to General Ord's command we had to cross the James in a boat, and then Mrs. Lincoln and Mrs. Grant got into the army ambulance as before, while Mrs. Ord and the gentlemen rode horseback. On the 27th General Sherman arrived, and there was a conference. The President was again much cheered by the confidence of both generals that they would be successful in speedily bringing the war to a close.

The next three days were filled with incidents. On one occasion the President, with General Grant,

Admiral Porter, Captain Penrose, Mrs. Lincoln, Taddie, and myself, went up the Appomattox to Point of Rocks, where we were rewarded by a view of the country for miles around. General Grant pointed out the location of General Lee's army; some of their tents were in full view. Near us, as we stood straining our eyes to see all we could of our Confederate adversaries, was a great oak-tree, said to mark the spot where Pocahontas saved the life of Captain John Smith. An inscription nailed to it—"Woodman, spare this tree"—gave us an idea of the respect due the patriarch. The best view was to be had from the "Crow's-nest"—a lookout tower constructed by General Butler when he was "bottled up" there earlier in the war. I think that the President really threw off the load that was on his mind and enjoyed the day. He said that he had, and looked pleased.

One day, while the President and Mrs. Lincoln were going through the hospital at City Point, doing what they could to cheer up the sick and wounded soldiers and investigating the hospital arrangements, some one told them that Mr. Johnson, the Vice-President, had arrived. Mr. Lincoln said: "Well, I guess he can get along without me." They did not meet at all during the visit. I do not know whether this meant that the President did not like Mr. Johnson or not. It may have been merely that he felt that he was at City Point for a certain purpose, and had no time for other things. The fact remains that he was not eager to see Mr. Johnson. The testimony of Major A. E. Johnson, who was Secretary Stanton's

THE ENTRANCE INTO RICHMOND

private secretary, is interesting in this connection. Major Johnson was present when the news came that Mr. Johnson had been chosen to be Mr. Lincoln's running-mate in the second election. He says that the President said: "So they have chosen him—I thought perhaps he would be the man. He is a strongman. I hope he may be the best man. But—" And, since the President rose then and went out of the room, the **but" was never explained.

The President made several trips up the James River to visit Admiral Porter and see his iron-clad fleet. One day he dined with him.

Not long before the final assault upon Petersburg a curious incident happened. A man came on board the River Queen and asked Captain Bradford if he could see the President. He was referred to me. Mr. Lincoln had instructed me not to admit any one but General Grant or Admiral Porter, so I told the man that the President was not to be seen. The visitor became very much excited. He said that he had rendered Mr. Lincoln valuable services in Illinois during his campaign for the Presidency, and had spent large sums of money. He was in trouble; he must see the President. He protested that he was known to Mr. Lincoln personally. I asked his name. At first he refused to give it, but finally said that it was "Smith" and that he lived near Mr. Lincoln's home in Illinois.

I went to the President and carried "Smith's" message. Mr. Lincoln laughed at first. "'Smith' is, of course, an uncommon name." Then he became serious. "If what he says is true, I would know him. But I do not. The man is an impostor, and I won't see him."

I went back to "Smith" with the President's answer. The man was very much disturbed, and again begged to be allowed to see him. When that failed he tried to bribe me to take him to Mr. Lincoln. I ordered him to leave the boat at once, and when he delayed told him I would have him arrested if he did not. He turned to Captain Bradford and said, defiantly, "If Mr. Lincoln does not know me now, he will know me damned soon after he does see me." He went on shore, and the moment after he had crossed the gangplank he disappeared. I watched him, but could not see where he had gone.

After the death of Mr. Lincoln, every one was anxious to discover the accomplices of the murderer. I called attention to this man " Smith" who had tried so hard to be admitted to Lincoln's presence at City Point. It was known that Surratt had been at City Point at that time, and I was requested to visit Surratt and see if I could identify him as "Smith." I went to court, and Taddie went with me. I had seen Surratt before the war; we had lived in the same county in Maryland. I think "Smith" and Surratt were the same man. It was impossible, however, for me to be absolutely sure. For "Smith" was ragged and dirty and very much sunburned; he looked like a tramp. While Surratt, at the time I saw him, looked like a very sick man, pale and emaciated. In every other respect they looked alike. The difference

THE ENTRANCE INTO RICHMOND

in appearance might easily have been brought about by circumstances or by a slight disguise. I shall always believe that Surratt was seeking an opportunity to assassinate the President at this time.

As March 31, 1865, drew near, the President (then at City Point, Virginia) knew that Grant was to make a general attack upon Petersburg, and grew depressed. The fact that his own son was with Grant was one source of anxiety. But the knowledge of the loss of life that must follow hung about him until he could think of nothing else. On the 31st there was, of course, no news. Most of the first day of April Mr. Lincoln spent in the telegraph-office, receiving telegrams and sending them on to Washington. Toward evening he came back to the River Queen, on which we had sailed from Washington to City Point.

There his anxiety became more intense. There had been a slight reverse during the day; he feared that the struggle might be prolonged. We could hear the cannon as they pounded away at Drury's Bluff up the river. We knew that not many miles away Grant was pouring fire into Lee's forces about Petersburg.

It grew dark. Then we could see the flash of the cannon. Mr. Lincoln would not go to his room. Almost all night he walked up and down the deck, pausing now and then to listen or to look out into the darkness to see if he could see anything. I have never seen such suffering in the face of any man as was in his that night.

On the morning of April 2d a message came from

General Grant asking the President to come to his headquarters, some miles distant from City Point and near Petersburg. It was on Sunday. We rode out to the intrenchments, close to the battle-ground. Mr. Lincoln watched the life-and-death struggle for some time, and then returned to City Point. In the evening he received a despatch from General Grant telling him that he had pushed Lee to his last lines about Petersburg. The news made the President happy. He said to Captain Penrose that the end of the war was now in sight. He could go to bed and sleep now. I remember how cheerful was his "Goodnight, Crook."

On Monday, the 3d, a message came to the President that Petersburg was in possession of the Federal army, and that General Grant was waiting there to see him. We mounted and rode over the battle-field to Petersburg. As we rode through Fort Hell and Fort Damnation—as the men had named the outposts of the two armies which faced each other, not far apart—many of the dead and dying were still on the ground. I can still see one man with a bullet-hole through his forehead, and another with both arms shot away. As we rode, the President's face settled into its old lines of sadness.

At the end of fifteen miles we reached Petersburg, and were met by Captain Robert Lincoln, of General Grant's staff, who, with some other officers, escorted us to General Grant. We found him and the rest of his staff sitting on the piazza of a white frame house. Grant did not look like one's idea of a conquering

THE ENTRANCE INTO RICHMOND

hero. He didn't appear exultant, and he was as quiet as he had ever been. The meeting between Grant and Lincoln was cordial; the President was almost affectionate. While they were talking I took the opportunity to stroll through Petersburg. It seemed deserted, but I met a few of the inhabitants. They said they were glad that the Union army had taken possession; they were half starved. They certainly looked so. The tobacco warehouses were on fire, and boys were carrying away tobacco to sell to the soldiers. I bought a five-pound bale of smokingtobacco for twenty-five cents. Just before we started back a little girl came up with a bunch of wild flowers for the President. He thanked the child for them kindly, and we rode away. Soon after we got back to City Point news came of the evacuation of Richmond.

In the midst of the rejoicing some Confederate prisoners were brought aboard transports at the dock near us. The President hung over the rail and watched them. They were in a pitiable condition, ragged and thin; they looked half starved. When they were on board they took out of their knapsacks the last rations that had been issued to them before capture. There was nothing but bread, which looked as if it had been mixed with tar. When they cut it we could see how hard and heavy it was; it was more like cheese than bread.

*' Poor fellows!" Mr. Lincoln said. *'It's a hard lot. Poor fellows—"

I looked up. His face was pitying and sorrowful. All the happiness had gone.

On the 4th of April Admiral Porter asked the President to go to Richmond with him. At first the President did not want to go. He knew it was foolhardy. And he had no wish to see the spectacle of the Confederacy's humiliation. It has been generally believed that it was Mr. Lincoln's own idea, and he has been blamed for rashness because of it. I understand that when Mr. Stanton, who was a vehement man, heard that the expedition had started, he was so alarmed that he was angry against the President. "That fool!" he exclaimed. Mr. Lincoln knew perfectly well how dangerous the trip was, and, as I said, at first he did not want to go, realizing that he had no right to risk his life unnecessarily. But he was convinced by Admiral Porter's arguments. Admiral Porter thought that the President ought to be in Richmond as soon after the surrender as possible. In that way he could gather up the reins of government most readily and give an impression of confidence in the South that would be helpful in the reorganization of the government. Mr. Lincoln immediately saw the wisdom of this position and went forward, calmly accepting the possibility of death.

Mrs. Lincoln, by this time, had gone back to Washington. Mr. Lincoln, Taddie, and I went up the James River on the River Queen to meet Admiral Porter's fleet. Taddie went down immediately to inspect the engine and talk with his friends the sailors; the President remained on deck. Near where Mr. Lincoln sat was a large bowl of apples on a table—there

THE ENTRANCE INTO RICHMOND

must have been at least half a peck. The President reached forward for one.

"These must have been put here for us," he said. "I guess I will sample them." We both began to pare and eat. Before we reached the Admiral's flagship every apple had disappeared—and the parings too. When the last one was gone the President said, with a smile, "I guess I have cleaned that fellow out."

When we met Admiral Porter's fleet the question of the best way to get to Richmond had to be decided. While some effort had been made to fish the torpedoes and other obstructions out of the water, but little headway had been made. The river was full of wreckage of all sorts, and torpedoes were floating everywhere. The plan had been to sail to Richmond in Admiral Porter's flag-ship *Malvern*, escorted by the Bat, and with the *Columbus* to carry the horses. But it was soon evident that it would not be possible to get as large a boat as the *Malvern* through at Drury's Bluff, where the naturally narrow and rapid channel was made impassable by a boat which had missed the channel and gone aground. It was determined to abandon the *Malvern* for the captain's gig, manned by twelve sailors. When the party, consisting of President Lincoln, Admiral Porter, Captain Penrose, Taddie, and myself, were seated, the *Bat*, a little tug which the President had used for his trips about City Point, came alongside and took us in tow. There were a number of marines on board the tug. We were kept at a safe distance from the tug by means of a long hawser, so that if she struck a torpedo and was blown up the President and his party would be safe. Even with this precaution the trip was exciting enough. On either side dead horses, broken ordnance, wrecked boats floated near our boat, and we passed so close to torpedoes that we could have put out our hands and touched them. We were dragged over one wreck which was so near the surface that it could be clearly seen.

Beyond Drury's Bluff, at a point where a bridge spans the water, the tug was sent back to help a steamboat which had stuck fast across the stream. It seems that it was the Allison, a captured Confederate vessel, and Admiral Farragut, who had taken it, was on board. The marines, of course, went with the tug. In the attempt to help the larger boat the tug was grounded. Then we went on with no other motive-power than the oars in the arms of the twelve sailors.

The shore for some distance before we reached Richmond was black with negroes. They had heard that President Lincoln was on his way—they had some sort of an underground telegraph, I am sure. They were wild with excitement, and yelling like so many wild men, "Dar comes Massa Linkum, de Sabier ob de lan'—we is so glad to see him!" We landed at the Rocketts, over a hundred yards back of Libby Prison. By the time we were on shore hundreds of black hands were outstretched to the President, and he shook some of them and thanked the darkies for their welcome. While we stood still a

THE ENTRANCE INTO RICHMOND

few minutes before beginning our walk through the city, we saw some soldiers not far away "initiating" some negroes by tossing them on a blanket. When they came down they were supposed to be transformed into Yankees. The darkies yelled lustily during the process, and came down livid under their black skins. But they were all eager for the ordeal. The President laughed boyishly; I heard him afterward telling some one about the funny sight.

We formed in line. Six sailors were in advance and six in the rear. They were armed with short carbines. Mr. Lincoln was in the centre, with Admiral Porter and Captain Penrose on the right, and I on the left, holding Taddie by the hand. I was armed with a Colt's revolver. We looked more like prisoners than anything else as we walked up the streets of Richmond not thirty-six hours after the Confederates had evacuated.

At first, except the blacks, there were not many people on the streets. But soon we were walking through streets that were alive with spectators. Wherever it was possible for a human being to find a foothold there was some man or woman or boy straining his eyes after the President. Every window was crowded with heads. Men were hanging from tree-boxes and telegraph-poles. But it was a silent crowd. There was something oppressive in those thousands of watchers without a sound, either of welcome or hatred. I think we would have welcomed a yell of defiance. I stole a look sideways at Mr. Lincoln. His face was set. It had the calm in it that comes over the face of a brave man when he is ready for whatever may come. In all Richmond the only sign of welcome I saw, after we left the negroes at the landing-place and until we reached our own men, was from a young lady who was on a sort of bridge that connected the Spottswood House with another hotel across the street. She had an American flag over her shoulders.

We had not gone far when the blinds of a second-story window of a house on our left were partly opened, and a man dressed in gray pointed something that looked like a gun directly at the President. I dropped Tad's hand and stepped in front of Mr. Lincoln. I was sure he meant to shoot. Later the President explained it otherwise. But we were all so aware of the danger of his entrance into Richmond right on the heels of the army, with such bitterness of feeling on the part of the Confederates, the streets swarming with disorderly characters, that our nerves were not steady. It seems to me nothing short of miraculous that some attempt on his life was not made. It is to the everlasting glory of the South that he was permitted to come and go in peace.

We were glad when we reached General Weitzel's headquarters in the abandoned Davis mansion and were at last among friends. Every one relaxed in the generous welcome of the General and his staff. The President congratulated General Weitzel, and a jubilation followed.

The Jefferson Davis home was a large house of gray stucco, with a garden at the back. It was a fine

THE ENTRANCE INTO RICHMOND

place, though everything looked dilapidated after the long siege. It was still completely furnished, and there was an old negro house-servant in charge. He told me that Mrs. Davis had ordered him to have the house in good condition for the Yankees.

" I am going out into the world a wanderer without a home," she had said when she bade him good-bye.

I was glad to know that he was to have everything "in good condition," for I was thirsty after so much excitement, and thought his orders must surely have included something to drink. I put the question to him. He said,

"Yes, indeed, boss, there is some fine old whiskey in the cellar."

In a few minutes he produced a long, black bottle. The bottle was passed around. When it came back it was empty. Every one had taken a pull except the President, who never touched anything of the sort.

An officer's ambulance was brought to the door, and President Lincoln, Admiral Porter, General Weitzel, with some of his staff, Captain Penrose, and Taddie took their seats. There was no room for me.

"Where is the place for Crook?" Mr. Lincoln asked. "I want him to go with me." Then they provided me with a saddle-horse, and I rode by the side on which Mr. Lincoln sat. We went through the city. Everywhere were signs of war, hundreds of homes had been fired, in some places buildings were still burning. It was with difficulty that we could get along, the crowd was so great. We passed Libby

Prison. The only place that we entered was the capitol. We were shown the room that had been occupied by Davis and his cabinet. The furniture was completely wrecked; the coverings of desks and chairs had been stripped off by relic-hunters, and the chairs were hacked to pieces.

The ambulance took us back to the wharf. Admiral Porter's flag-ship Malvern had by this time made her way up the river, and we boarded her. It was with a decided feeling of relief that we saw the President safe on board.

We did not start back until the next morning, so there was time for several rumors of designs against the President's life to get abroad. But although he saw many visitors, there was no attempt against him. Nothing worse happened than the interview with Mr. Duff Green.

Duff Green was a conspicuous figure at the time. He was a newspaper man, an ardent rebel. He always carried with him a huge staff, as tall as he was himself—and he was a tall man. Admiral Porter published an account of the interview in the New York Tribune of January, 1885, which was not altogether accurate. What really happened was this:

As Mr. Green approached him, the President held out his hand. Mr. Green refused to take it, saying, "I did not come to shake hands." Mr. Lincoln then sat down; so did Mr. Green. There were present at the time General Weitzel, Admiral Porter, one or two others, and myself. Mr. Green began to abuse Mr. Lincoln for the part he had taken in the struggle

THE ENTRANCE INTO RICHMOND

between the North and the South. His last words were,

" I do not know how God and your conscience will let you sleep at night after being guilty of the notorious crime of setting the niggers free."

The President listened to his diatribe without the slightest show of emotion. He said nothing. There was nothing in his face to show that he was angry. When Mr. Green had exhausted himself, he said,

"I would like, sir, to go to my friends."

The President turned to General Weitzel and said, "General, please give Mr. Green a pass to go to his friends." Mr. Green was set ashore, and was seen no more.

That night Taddie and I were fast asleep when I was startled into wakefulness. Something tall and white and ghostly stood by my berth. For a moment I trembled. When I was fairly awake I saw that it was Mr. Lincoln in his long, white nightgown. He had come in to see if Taddie was all right. He stopped to talk a few minutes.

He referred to Mr. Duff Green: "The old man is pretty angry, but I guess he will get over it." Then he said, "Good-night, and a good night's rest. Crook," and he went back to his stateroom.

Our return trip to City Point was in the Malvern, and quiet enough in comparison with the approach to Richmond. When we reached the "Dutch Gap Canal," which was one of the engineering features of the day, the President wanted to go through it. Admiral Porter lowered a boat, and in it we passed through the canal to the James below. The canal cuts off a long loop of the river. We had to wait some time for the *Malvern* to go around.

Mrs. Lincoln had returned to City Point with a party which included Senator Sumner and Senator and Mrs. Harlan. They made a visit to Richmond, accompanied by Captain Penrose, while the President remained at City Point, the guest of Admiral Porter, until the 8th. Then, having heard of the injury to Secretary Seward when he was thrown from his carriage in a runaway accident, he felt that he must go back to Washington. He had intended to remain until Lee surrendered.

We reached home Sunday evening, the 9th. The President's carriage met us at the wharf. There Mr. Lincoln parted from Captain Penrose; he took the captain by the hand and thanked him for the manner in which he had performed his duty. Then he started for the White House.

The streets were alive with people, all very much excited. There were bonfires everywhere. We were all curious to know what had happened. Tad was so excited he couldn't keep still. We halted the carriage and asked a bystander,

"What has happened?"

He looked at us in amazement, not recognizing Mr. Lincoln.

" Why, where have you been ? Lee has surrendered."

There is one point which is not understood, I think, about the President's trip to City Point and Rich-

THE ENTRANCE INTO RICHMOND

mond. I would like to tell here what my experience has made me believe. The expedition has been spoken of almost as if it were a pleasure trip. Some one says of it, "It was the first recreation the President had known." Of course, in one sense this was true. He did get away from the routine of office-work. He had pleasant associations with General Grant and General Sherman, and enjoyed genial talks in the open over the camp-fire. But to give the impression that it was a sort of holiday excursion is a mistake. It was a matter of executive duty, and a very trying and saddening duty in many of its features. The President's suspense during the days when he knew the battle of Petersburg was imminent, his agony when the thunder of the cannon told him that men were being cut down like grass, his sight of the poor, torn bodies of the dead and dying on the field of Petersburg, his painful sympathy with the forlorn rebel prisoners, the revelation of the devastation of a noble people in ruined Richmond—these things may have been compensated for by his exultation when he first knew the long struggle was over. But I think not. These things wore new furrows in his face. Mr. Lincoln never looked sadder in his life than when he walked through the streets of Richmond and knew it saved to the Union and himself victorious.

IV

A NEW PHASE OF THE ASSASSINATION

ALTHOUGH I reported early at the White House . on the morning after our return from City Point, I found the President already at his desk. He was looking over his mail, but as I came in he looked up, and said, pleasantly:

"Good-morning, Crook. How do you feel?"

I answered: "First-rate, Mr. President. How are you?"

"I am well, but rather tired," he said.

Then I noticed that he did, indeed, look tired. His worn face made me understand, more clearly than I had done before, what a strain the experiences at Petersburg and Richmond had been. Now that the excitement was over, the reaction allowed it to be seen.

I was on duty near the President all that day. We settled back into the usual routine. It seemed odd to go on as if nothing had happened; the trip had been such a great event. It was a particularly busy day. Correspondence had been held for Mr. Lincoln's attention during the seventeen days of absence; besides that, his office was thronged with visitors. Some of them had come to congratulate him on the

NEW PHASE OF THE ASSASSINATION

successful outcome of the war; others had come to advise him what course to pursue toward the conquered Confederacy; still others wanted appointments. One gentleman, who was bold enough to ask aloud what everybody was asking privately, said,

"Mr. President, what will you do with Jeff Davis when he is caught?"

Mr. Lincoln sat up straight and crossed his legs, as he always did when he was going to tell a story.

"Gentlemen," he said, "that reminds me"—at the familiar words every one settled back and waited for the story—"that reminds me of an incident which occurred in a little town in Illinois where I once practised law. One morning I was on my way to the office, when I saw a boy standing on the street corner crying. I felt sorry for the woebegone little fellow. So I stopped and questioned him as to the cause of his grief. He looked into my face, the tears running down his cheeks, and said: 'Mister, do you see that coon?'—pointing to a very poor specimen of the coon family which glared at us from the end of the string. 'Well, sir, that coon has given me a heap of trouble. He has nearly gnawed the string in two—I just wish he would finish it. Then I could go home and say he had got away.'"

Everybody laughed. They all knew quite well what the President would like to do with Jeff Davis —when Jeff Davis was caught.

Later in the morning a great crowd came marching into the White House grounds. Every man was cheering and a band was playing patriotic airs. The workmen at the Navy-Yard had started the procession, and by the time it had reached us it was over two thousand strong. Of course they called for the President, and he stepped to the window to see his guests. When the cheering had subsided he spoke to them very kindly and good-naturedly, begging that they would not ask him for a serious speech.

"I am going to make a formal address this evening," he said, "and if I dribble it out to you now, my speech to-night will be spoiled." Then, with his humorous smile, he spoke to the band:

"I think it would be a good plan for you to play Dixie. I always thought that it was the most beautiful of our songs. I have submitted the question of its ownership to the Attorney-General, and he has given it as his legal opinion that we have fairly earned the right to have it back." As the opening bars of Dixie burst out, Mr. Lincoln disappeared from the window. The crowed went off in high good-humor, marching to the infectious rhythm of the hard-won tune.

On the afternoon of the same day, about six o'clock, a deputation of fifteen men called. Mr. Lincoln met them in the corridor just after they had entered the main door. They were presented to the President, and then the gentleman who had introduced them made a speech. It was a very pretty speech, full of loyal sentiments and praise for the man who had safely guided the country through the great crisis. Mr. Lincoln listened to them pleasantly.

NEW PHASE OF THE ASSASSINATION

Then a picture was put into his hands. When he saw his own rugged features facing him from an elaborate silver frame a smile broadened his face.

"Gentlemen," he said, "I thank you for this token of your esteem. You did your best. It wasn't your fault that the frame is so much more rare than the picture."

On the evening of the nth the President made the speech which he had promised the day before. Had we only known it, this was to be his last public utterance. The whole city was brilliantly illuminated that night. The public buildings were decorated, and, from the Capitol to the Treasury, the whole length of Pennsylvania Avenue bore witness, with flags and lights, to the joy everybody felt because the war was over. Streaming up Pennsylvania Avenue, which was the one great thoroughfare then, the only paved street, and from every other quarter of the city, came the people. In spite of the unpleasant drizzle which fell the whole evening, and the mud through which every one had to wade, a great crowd cheered Mr. Lincoln when he appeared at an upper window. From another window Mrs. Lincoln bowed to the people and was greeted enthusiastically. The President immediately began his speech, which had been in preparation ever since his return from City Point. The care which he had taken to express himself accurately was shown from the fact that the whole address was written out. Inside, little Tad was running around the room while "papa-day" was speaking. As the President let the sheets of manuscript fall, Taddie gathered them up and begged his father to let them go faster.

The President spoke with reverence of the cause for thanksgiving that the long struggle was over. He passed rapidly to that question which he knew the whole nation was debating—the future policy toward the South. In discussing his already much-debated "Louisiana Policy" he expressed the two great principles which were embodied in it: the mass of the Southern people should be restored to their citizenship as soon as it was evident that they desired it; punishment, *if punishment there be*, should fall upon those who had been proved to be chiefly instrumental in leading the South into rebellion. These principles were reiterated by Senator Harlan, the Secretary of the Interior to be, who spoke after the President; they were reiterated, of course, by the President's desire. During President Andrew Johnson's long struggle with a bitter Northern Congress, I have often recalled the simplicity and kindliness of Abraham Lincoln's theory.

During the next three days—as, in fact, since the fall of Richmond—Washington was a little delirious. Everybody was celebrating. The kind of celebration depended on the kind of person. It was merely a question of whether the intoxication was mental or physical. Every day there was a stream of callers who came to congratulate the President, to tell how loyal they had been, and how they had always been sure he would be victorious. There were serenades; there were deputations of leading citizens; on the

NEW PHASE OF THE ASSASSINATION

evening of the 13th there was another illumination. The city became disorderly with the men who were celebrating too hilariously. Those about the President lost somewhat of the feeling, usually present, that his life was not safe. It did not seem possible that, now that the war was over and the government—glad to follow General Grant's splendid initiative—had been so magnanimous in its treatment of General Lee, after President Lincoln had offered himself a target for Southern bullets in the streets of Richmond and had come out unscathed, there could be danger. For my part, I had drawn a full breath of relief after we got out of Richmond, and had forgotten to be anxious since.

Because of the general joyousness, I was surprised when, late on the afternoon of the 14th, I accompanied Mr. Lincoln on a hurried visit to the War Department, I found that the President was more depressed than I had ever seen him and his step unusually slow. Afterward Mrs. Lincoln told me that when he drove with her to the Soldiers' Home earlier in the afternoon he had been extremely cheerful, even buoyant. She said that he had talked of the calm future that was in store for them, of the ease which they had never known, when, his term over, they would go back to their home in Illinois. He longed, a little wistfully, for that time to come, with its promise of peace. The depression I noticed may have been due to one of the sudden changes of mood to which I have been told the President was subject. I had heard of the transitions from almost wild spirits to abject melan choly which marked him. I had never seen anything of the sort, and had concluded that all this must have belonged to his earlier days. In the time when I knew him his mood, when there was no outside sorrow to disturb him, was one of settled calm. I wondered at him that day and felt uneasy.

In crossing over to the War Department we passed some drunken men. Possibly their violence suggested the thought to the President. After we had passed them, Mr. Lincoln said to me,

"Crook, do you know, I believe there are men who want to take my life ?" Then, after a pause, he said, half to himself, "And I have no doubt they will do it."

The conviction with which he spoke dismayed me. I wanted to protest, but his tone had been so calm and sure that I found myself saying, instead, "Why do you think so, Mr. President?"

"Other men have been assassinated," was his reply, still in that manner of stating something to himself.

All I could say was, "I hope you are mistaken, Mr. President."

We walked a few paces in silence. Then he said, in a more ordinary tone:

" I have perfect confidence in those who are around me—in every one of you men. I know no one could do it and escape alive. But if it is to be done, it is impossible to prevent it."

By this time we were at the War Department, and he went in to his conference with Secretary Stan-

NEW PHASE OF THE ASSASSINATION

ton. It was shorter than usual that evening. Mr. Lincoln had been belated. When Mrs. Lincoln and he came home from their drive he had found friends awaiting him. He had slipped away from dinner, and there were more people waiting to talk to him when he got back. He came out of the Secretary's office in a short time. Then I saw that every trace of the depression, or perhaps I should say intense seriousness, which had surprised me before had vanished. He talked to me as usual. He said that Mrs. Lincoln and he, with a party, were going to the theatre to see Our American Cousin.

"It has been advertised that we will be there," he said, "and I cannot disappoint the people. Otherwise I would not go. I do not want to go."

I remember particularly that he said this, because it surprised me. The President's love for the theatre was well known. He went often when it was announced that he would be there; but more often he would slip away, alone or with Tad, get into the theatre, unobserved if he could, watch the play from the back of the house for a short time, and then go back to his work. Mr. Buckingham, the doorkeeper of Ford's Theatre, used to say that he went in just to "take a laugh." So it seemed unusual to hear him say he did not want to go. When we had reached the White House and he had climbed the steps he turned and stood there a moment before he went in. Then he said,

"Good-bye, Crook."

It startled me. As far as I remember he had never

said anything but "Good-night, Crook," before. Of course, it is possible that I may be mistaken. In looking back, every word that he said has significance. But I remember distinctly the shock of surprise and the impression, at the time, that he had never said it before.

By this time I felt queer and sad. I hated to leave him. But he had gone in, so I turned away and started on my walk home. I lived in a little house on "Rodbird's Hill." It was a long distance from the White House—it would be about on First Street now, in the middle of the block between L and M Streets. The whole tract from there to North Capitol Street belonged either to my father-in-law or to his family. He was an old, retired sea-captain named Rodbird; he had the hull of his last sailing-vessel set up in his front-yard.

The feeling of sadness with which I left the President lasted a long time, but wore off after a while—I was young and healthy, I was going home to my wife and baby, and, the man who followed me on duty having been late for some reason, it was long past my usual dinner-time, and I was hungry. By the time I had had my dinner I was sleepy, so I went to bed early. I did not hear until early in the morning that the President had been shot. It seems incredible now, but it was so.

My first thought was, If I had been on duty at the theatre, I would be dead now. My next was to wonder whether Parker, who had gone to the theatre with the President, was dead. Then I remembered

NEW PHASE OF THE ASSASSINATION

what the President had said the evening before. Then I went to the house on Tenth Street where they had taken him.

They would not let me in. The little room where he lay was crowded with the men who had been associated with the President during the war. They were gathered around the bed watching, while, long after the great spirit was quenched, life, little by little, loosened its hold on the long, gaunt body. Among them, I knew, were men who had contended with him during his life or who had laughed at him. Charles Sumner stood at the very head of the bed. I know that it was to him that Robert Lincoln, who was only a boy for all his shoulder-straps, turned in the long strain of watching. And on Charles Sumner's shoulder the son sobbed out his grief. But the room was full, and they would not let me in.

After the President had died they took him back to the White House. It was to the guest-room, with its old four-posted bed, that they carried him. I was in the room while the men prepared his body to be seen by his people when they came to take their leave. It was hard for me to be there. It seemed fitting that the body should be there, where he had never been in life. I am glad that his own room could be left to the memory of his living presence.

The days during which the President lay in state before they took him away for his long progress over the country he had saved were even more distressing than grief would have made them. Mrs. Lincoln was almost frantic with suffering. Women spiritualists in some way gained access to her. They poured into her ears pretended messages from her dead husband. Mrs. Lincoln was so weakened that she had not force enough to resist the cruel cheat. These women nearly crazed her. Mr. Robert Lincoln, who had to take his place now at the head of the family, finally ordered them out of the house.

After the President's remains were taken from the White House the family began preparations for leaving, but they were delayed a month by Mrs. Lincoln's illness. The shock of her husband's death had brought about a nervous disorder. Her physiccian, Doctor Stone, refused to allow her to be moved until she was somewhat restored. During the whole of the time while she was shut up in her room Mrs. Gideon Welles, the wife of the Secretary of the Navy, was in almost daily attendance upon her. Mrs. Welles was Mrs. Lincoln's friend, of all the women in official position, and she did much with her kindly ministrations to restore the President's widow to her normal condition. It was not until the 23d of May, at six o'clock, that Mrs. Lincoln finally left for Chicago.

Capt. Robert Lincoln accompanied her, and a colored woman, a seamstress, in whom she had great confidence, went with the party to act as Mrs. Lincoln's maid. They asked me to go with them to do what I could to help. But no one could do much for Mrs. Lincoln. During most of the fifty-four hours that we were on the way she was in a daze; it seemed almost a stupor. She hardly spoke. No one could get near enough to her grief to comfort her. But I could be of some use to Taddie. Being a child, he had been able to cry away some of his grief, and he could be distracted with the sights out of the car-window. There was an observation-car at the end of our coach. Taddie and I spent a good deal of time there, looking at the scenes flying past. He began to ask questions.

It had been expected that Mrs. Lincoln would go back to her old home in Illinois. But she did not seem to be able to make up her mind to go there. She remained for some time in Chicago at the old Palmer House.

I went to a friend who had gone from Washington to Chicago to live, and remained with him for the week I was in the city. I went to the hotel every day. Mrs. Lincoln I rarely saw. Taddie I took out for a walk almost every day and tried to interest him in the sights we saw. But he was a sad little fellow, and mourned for his father.

At last I went back to Washington and to the White House. President Johnson had established his offices there when I got back.

Now that I have told the story of my three months' association with Abraham Lincoln, there are two things of which I feel that I must speak. The first question relates to the circumstances of the assassination of President Lincoln. It has never been made public before.

I have often wondered why the negligence of the

guard who accompanied the President to the theatre on the night of the 14th has never been divulged. So far as I know, it was not even investigated by the police department. Yet, had he done his duty, I believe President Lincoln would not have been murdered by Booth. The man was John Parker. He was a native of the District, and had volunteered, as I believe each of the other guards had done, in response to the President's first call for troops from the District. He is dead now, and, as far as I am able to discover, all of his family. So it is no unkindness to speak of the costly mistake he made.

It was the custom for the guard who accompanied the President to the theatre to remain in the little passageway outside the box—that passageway through which Booth entered. Mr. Buckingham, who was the doorkeeper at Ford's Theatre, remembers that a chair was placed there for the guard on the evening of the 14th. Whether Parker occupied it at all I do not know—Mr. Buckingham is of the impression that he did. If he did, he left it almost immediately; for he confessed to me the next day that he went to a seat at the front of the first gallery, so that he could see the play. The door of the President's box was shut; probably Mr. Lincoln never knew that the guard had left his post.

Mr. Buckingham tells that Booth was in and out of the house five times before he finally shot the President. Each time he looked about the theatre in a restless, excited manner. I think there can be no doubt that he was studying the scene of his in tended crime, and that he observed that Parker, whom he must have been watching, was not at his post. To me it is very probable that the fact that there was no one on guard may have determined the time of his attack. Booth had found it necessary to stimulate himself with whiskey in order to reach the proper pitch of fanaticism. Had he found a man at the door of the President's box armed with a Colt's revolver, his alcohol courage might have evaporated.

However that may be, Parker's absence had much to do with the success of Booth's purpose. The assassin was armed with a dagger and a pistol. The story used to be that the dagger was intended for General Grant when the President had been despatched. That is absurd. While it had been announced that General and Mrs. Grant would be in the box, Booth, during one of his five visits of inspection, had certainly had an opportunity to observe that the General was absent. The dagger, which was noiseless, was intended for any one who might intercept him before he could fire. The pistol, which was noisy and would arouse pursuit, was for the President. As it happened, since the attack was a complete surprise, Major Rathbone, who, the President having been shot, attempted to prevent Booth's escape, received the dagger in his arm.

Had Parker been at his post at the back of the box —Booth still being determined to make the attempt that night—he would have been stabbed, probably killed. The noise of the struggle—Parker could surely have managed to make some outcry—would have given the alarm. Major Rathbone was a brave man, and the President was a brave man and of enormous muscular strength. It would have been an easy thing for the two men to have disarmed Booth, who was not a man of great physical strength. It was the suddenness of his attack on the President that made it so devilishly successful. It makes me feel rather bitter when I remember that the President had said, just a few hours before, that he knew he could trust all his guards. And then to think that in that one moment of test one of us should have utterly failed him! Parker knew that he had failed in duty. He looked like a convicted criminal the next day. He was never the same man afterward.

The other fact that I think people should know has been stated before in the President's own words: President Lincoln believed that it was probable he would be assassinated.

The conversation that I had with him on the 14th was not the only one we had on that same subject. Any one can see how natural it was that the matter should have come up between us—my very presence beside him was a reminder that there was danger of assassination. In his general kindliness he wanted to talk about the thing that constituted my own particular occupation. He often spoke of the possibility of an attempt being made on his life. With the exception of that last time, however, he never trea-ted it very seriously. He merely expressed the general idea that, I afterward learned, he had expressed to Marshal Lamon and other men: if any one was willing to give his own life in the attempt to murder the President, it would be impossible to prevent him.

On that last evening he went further. He said with conviction that he believed that the men who wanted to take his life would do it. As far as I know, I am the only person to whom President Lincoln made such a statement. He may possibly have spoken about it to the other guards, but I never heard of it, and I am sure that had he done so I would have known it.

More than this, I believe that he had some vague sort of a warning that the attempt would be made on the night of the 14th. I know that this is an extraordinary statement to make, and that it is late in the day to make it. I have been waiting for just the proper opportunity to say this thing; I did not care to talk idly about it. I would like to give my reasons for feeling as I do. The chain of circumstances is at least an interesting thing to consider.

It is a matter of record that on the morning of the 14th, at a cabinet meeting, the President spoke of the recurrence the night before of a dream which, he said, had always forerun something of moment in his life. In the dream a ship under full sail bore down upon him. At the time he spoke of it he felt that some good fortune was on its way to him. He was serene, even joyous, over it. Later in the day, while he was driving with his wife, his mind still seemed to be dwelling on the question of the future. It was their future together of which he spoke. He was almost impatient that his term should be over. He seemed eager for rest and peace. When I accompanied him to the War Department, he had become depressed and spoke of his belief that he would be assassinated. When we returned to the White House, he said that he did not want to go to the theatre that evening, but that he must go so as not to disappoint the people. In connection with this it is to be remembered that he was extremely fond of the theatre, and that the bill that evening, Our American Cousin, was a very popular one. When he was about to enter the White House he said "Good-bye," as I never remember to have heard him say before when I was leaving for the night.

These things have a curious interest. President Lincoln was a man of entire sanity. But no one has ever sounded the spring of spiritual insight from which his nature was fed. To me it all means that he had, with his waking on that day, a strong prescience of coming change. As the day wore on the feeling darkened into an impression of coming evil. The suggestion of the crude violence we witnessed on the street pointed to the direction from which that evil should come. He was human; he shrank from it. But he was characterized by what some men call fatalism; others, devotion to duty; still others, religious faith. Therefore he went open-eyed to the place where he met, at last, the blind fanatic. And in that meeting the President, who had dealt out justice with a tender heart, who had groaned in spirit over fallen Richmond, fell.

NEW PHASE OF THE ASSASSINATION

More and more persons who have heard that I was with Mr. Lincoln come to me asking,

"What was he like?"

These last years, when, at a Lincoln birthday celebration or some other memorial gathering, they ask for a few words from the man who used to be Abraham Lincoln's guard, the younger people look at me as if I were some strange spectacle—a man who lived by Lincoln's side. It has made me feel as if the time had come when I ought to tell the world the little that I know about him. Soon there will be nothing of him but the things that have been written.

Yet, when I try to say what sort of a man he seemed to me, I fail. I have no words. All I can do is to give little snatches of reminiscences—I cannot picture the man. I can say:

He is the only man I ever knew the foundation of whose spirit was love. That love made him suffer. I saw him look at the ragged, hungry prisoners at City Point, I saw him ride over the battle-fields at Petersburg, the man with the hole in his forehead and the man with both arms shot away lying, accusing, before his eyes. I saw him enter into Richmond, walking between lanes of silent men and women who had lost their battle. I remember his face. . . .And yet my memory of him is not of an unhappy man. I hear so much to-day about the President's melancholy. It is true no man could suffer more. But he was very easily amused. I have never seen a man who enjoyed more anything pleasant or funny that came his way. I think the balance between pain and pleasure was fairly struck, and in the last months when I knew him he was in love with life because he found it possible to do so much. . . . I never saw evidence of faltering. I do not believe any one ever did. From the moment he, who was all pity, pledged himself to war, he kept straight on.

I can follow Secretary John Hay and say, He was the greatest man I have ever known—or shall ever know.

That ought to be enough to say, and yet—nothing so merely of words seems to express him. Something that he did tells so much more.

I remember one afternoon, not long before the President was shot, we were on our way to the War Department, when we passed a ragged, dirty man in army clothes lounging just outside the White House enclosure. He had evidently been waiting to see the President, for he jumped up and went toward him with his story. He had been wounded, was just out of the hospital—he looked forlorn enough. There was something he wanted the President to do; he had papers with him. Mr. Lincoln was in a hurry, but he put out his hands for the papers. Then he sat down on the curbstone, the man beside him, and examined them. When he had satisfied himself about the matter, he smiled at the anxious fellow reassuringly and told him to come back the next day; then he would arrange the matter for him. A thing like that says more than any man could express. If I could only make people see him as I did—see how simple he was with every one; how he could talk with a child so

NEW PHASE OF THE ASSASSINATION

that the child could understand and smile up at him; how you would never know, from his manner to the plainest or poorest or meanest, that there was the least difference between that man and himself; how, from that man to the greatest, and all degrees between, the President could meet every man square on the plane where he stood and speak to him, man to man, from that plane—if I could do that, I would feel that I had told something of what he was. For no one to whom he spoke with his perfect simplicity ever presumed to answer him familiarly, and I never saw him stand beside any man—and I saw him with the greatest men of the day—that I did not feel there again President Lincoln was supreme. If I had only words to tell what he seemed to me!

V

ANDREW JOHNSON IN THE WHITE HOUSE

WHEN I left Washington to accompany Mrs. Lincoln and Tad on their journey back to Illinois, the new President was occupying temporary offices in the west front of the Treasury Building. On my return, I found that he had moved into the White House. He did not, however, take Mr. Lincoln's old office for his own use. Because of the larger office force, a change in the arrangement was necessary, and Mr. Lincoln's room was used by clerks. The President had his desk in the former anteroom, which had been enlarged by taking away the partition used by Mr. Lincoln to give him private access to the library. Mr. Johnson's secretaries worked in the corner room which we had become accustomed to associate with Mr. Nicolay and Mr. Hay.

I must admit that it was a relief to me not to see Mr. Johnson in the familiar corner of the office from which for so many days Mr. Lincoln's deep eyes had smiled a kindly good-morning. The new President was different from the dead President, whom we missed every day. Even in his appearance he was as great a contrast to Mr. Lincoln as was possible where two men are of the same country, the same period, and of somewhat the same class. He was short, while Mr. Lincoln was remarkably tall; he was burly, while Mr. Lincoln was gaunt. With his black hair and eyes and Indian-like swarthiness, he had an Indian-like impassiveness of expression. There were none of the lines in his face which, with Mr. Lincoln, showed just how many times he had laughed and how many times he had grieved. Instead of these, there were two lines of decision drawn from the corners of his mouth, and two from his nose. A strong nose and a square chin jutted toward each other from obstinate angles. Very few persons got beyond these things, and saw that he had a cleft in his chin. I know I did not for a long time; I imagine the women and children were quicker.

Even at that time Mr. Johnson was an unpopular man, and I shared in the common prejudice against him. Even before that April day when, in gloomy haste, he had taken the oath of office, circumstances determined that his position would be a difficult one. He had been thrust into responsibilities and honors to which no man had dreamed of his succeeding; his nomination to the Vice-Presidency had been a political accident. He was from the South, and had profited by the crime of a Southerner—a crime which had destroyed the one who, at the time of his death, was the best-loved man in the country. His origin and early conditions had been sordid, and of this sordidness he was entirely unashamed. Neither thing helped his position with a narrow circle of New England theorists who, with their inheritance of inflated ideals and incomplete sympathies, had come to replace, by way of aristocracy, the social traditions of colonial times.

In addition, there were certain drawbacks of a more personal nature. The unfortunate circumstances of his inauguration as Vice-President were fresh in people's minds. It had been currently reported that on that occasion Mr. Johnson was intoxicated. He had certainly acted in a manner to offend the men who were about him and to lower the Vice-President before his subordinates. Since then the matter has been explained. We all know now that he was then recovering from a severe attack of typhoid-fever. He was not in a condition to go through even the simple ceremonial which marked Mr. Lincoln's second inauguration. In order that he might be able to perform his part in the exercises of the day, he had taken a stimulant. The effect of alcohol upon typhoid convalescents is well known, the smallest amount being intoxicating. This incident brought about a reputation for drunkenness which clung to the President throughout his administration. The slander was used by Mr. Johnson's enemies for their own purposes. To offset these disadvantages, there was nothing in Mr. Johnson's self-contained, almost sombre manner to take possession of the hearts of those about him, as did the man with whom we were forced to compare him.

But I had not been many days about the White House before I began to change my opinion of Andrew Johnson. My prejudices against him began to die

ANDREW JOHNSON

JOHNSON IN THE WHITE HOUSE

away. I grew to follow his directions with alacrity and to welcome his rare and laconic remarks. I was not alone in this change: all of the employees began to feel his influence. He was a man who, through association, swayed insensibly the men who were with him. I very soon began to realize that the reports of his drinking to excess were, like many other slanders, without foundation. I will state here that during the years he was in the White House there never was any foundation for it. Except in the time of his absence in the autumn of 1865, I saw him probably every day, from the time of my return until he left, and I never once saw him under the influence of liquor. With regard to his life before and after this period, of course I can offer no direct testimony; but I have heard the indignant denials of the men who were associated with him. For my part, the record of his energetic and forceful life would be proof enough for me, even if I did not know from my own observation. No man whose wits were fuddled with alcohol could have done what he did in Tennessee and Washington. He drank, as did virtually most public men of the time, a notable exception being Mr. Lincoln. The White House cellars were well stocked with wine and whiskies, which he offered to his guests at dinner or luncheon, but in my experience he never drank to excess.

I learned another thing, too, and that was that the President was destined to conflict. He was a man who found it impossible to conciliate or temporize. As uncompromising as the terms of his speech, as straight as the challenge of his eye, Andrew Johnson's opinions and policies did not change. His goal being ahead of him, and seen in clear light, he neither saw nor considered possible an indirect path to that goal. It was inevitable, when other men were going in opposite ways, that there should be collision.

There was nothing of this conflict apparent at first, however- for there were practical details to absorb him. Mr. Johnson was a hard-working and businesslike man. Except for an hour or so in the afternoon and at meal-times, he rarely left his desk until midnight. He immediately went to work to organize an executive office, which had never been done before. This was imperative, because of the mass of details caused by the end of the war. The numerous exceptions to the Amnesty Proclamation, embracing the cases of the men who had been the leaders of the Confederacy and all men possessing $20,000 or more of property, made it necessary to grant a great many pardons. At the beginning of his administration the President was prejudiced against the natural leaders, who, he considered, had led the South astray. The $20,000 exception to the first Amnesty Proclamation was his own idea, introduced because of his prejudice against aristocrats and in favor of the "plain people." It was generally expected that he would prove severe in his attitude toward the excepted classes; but he merely wished to make their probation long enough to enforce the lesson of loyalty upon them. Therefore the granting of pardons became part of the routine of office. From April 15, 1865, to June 15,

1866, I have been told that 1963 pardons were granted. It is easy to see how much clerical work this matter alone entailed.

Mr. Johnson employed six secretaries, instead of two, as Mr. Lincoln had done. They were classified as one secretary and one assistant secretary, with the others detailed from the War Department. At the beginning, William H, Browning was the secretary, and Robert Morrow the assistant. Mr. Browning did not serve long, however. When he died, the President's son, Colonel Robert Johnson, took his place. For a time Mr. Cooper, representative-elect from Tennessee, while waiting the decision of Congress relative to the readmission of Tennessee, served as secretary. Colonel Long, Colonel Wright Reeves, Major William C. Moore, and General Mussey were detailed from the War Department. For a long time Colonel Long had charge of the business of pardons.

Besides the private secretaries, Mr. Johnson had six clerks detailed from the departments to assist in the work of the office. These, as I said, were stationed in Mr. Lincoln's old room. For the first time in the history of the White House, records of the office were kept. There had never been anything before but lists of appointments. The books would repay any one's study. A small one which I have chanced to retain contains the first records of the case against the conspirators implicated with Booth in the murder of President Lincoln. In it Mr. Johnson submitted this question to the Secretary of War, Should the trial be delegated to a military tribunal ? There are references to manuscripts in the case. Everything shows a painstaking desire to understand thoroughly the details. There is evidence, too, of a wish to consider the authority of the Secretary of War. One amusing entry in the book is the plea of an Episcopalian minister who, too evidently disapproving, desired to be released from his obligation to pray for the President of the United States.

Mr. Johnson not only kept this official account of his actions, but preserved every letter of his correspondence. He had scrap-books of newspaper clippings compiled. After a time these were my special charge. All this material—records, correspondence, scrap-books—is now in the Manuscript Division of the Congressional Library at Washington. It is possible to see there, side by side with receipts for hats and shoes, and pink leaflets containing the Sunday-school lessons of small grandchildren, the gravest political documents.

It was August, and the routine of the office was fairly under way, when the White House finally became the home of all the President's family. There were Mrs. Johnson; Colonel Robert Johnson, the President's second son; Senator Patterson and his wife, who was the eldest daughter, with her children, Belle and Andrew; Mrs. Stover, a widow, with her three children, Lillie, Sarah, and Andrew. There was also a young son of the President, Andrew, who was sometimes called Frank, to lessen the confusion arising from the other two young Andrews. The eldest son, Charles, who had been a surgeon in the army, had died before this time. The White House has never been so full of children. They were an important interest in the President's life.

Mrs. Johnson was so much of an invalid that outside of intimate family friends very few knew her. She appeared only twice in public during her husband's administration. Still, her influence was a strong one, and it was exerted in the direction of toleration and gentleness. A slight movement of her hands, a touch on her husband's arm, a "Now, Andrew," made it easy to see that the woman who had helped him through his struggling youth and given her health to his service, who had taught him to write and had read to him through long winter evenings in the little tailor-shop that his active mind might be fed while he was practising his trade, still held her place in his life. She was a sweet-faced woman, who showed traces of beauty through the sharpened lines caused by the old-fashioned consumption which was wearing her out. Her face was not unlike that of the late Mrs. McKinley. The death of her eldest son was a blow from which she never fully recovered. The life in Washington was not a happy time for her. She told me herself that she was far more content when her husband was an industrious young tailor.

Mrs. Stover was not at the White House during the whole of her father's term, and Mrs. Patterson was the real mistress of the establishment. No woman could have acted with greater sense or discretion. She had passed her girlhood days in Washington, had been educated at a school in Georgetown, and during the Polk administration had been a frequent guest at the White House, so she was not entirely unfamiliar with official life in the capital. She made no pretences of any sort, but was always honest and direct. She said to a lady who called upon her soon after she came to the White House, "You mustn't expect too much of us; we are only plain people from Tennessee." The very modesty of this statement is misleading. It is true that the Johnsons did not pretend to be leaders in the social life of Washington, and in their regime there was no joyousness, no special grace, in the White House festivities; there was, however, exactness in the discharge of social duties, and a homely dignity, equally free from ostentation and undue humility. The dinners and public receptions were more numerous than under Johnson's successors, and they were not lacking in brilliancy. Mr. Johnson quite understood the value and place of social functions.

The first public duty that confronted Mr. Johnson was the punishment of those who, together with Booth, had conspired to murder the late President and his cabinet. The question of the tribunal had first to be decided. Attorney-General Speed gave it as his opinion that it would be proper to confide the trial to a military court. The President submitted the matter to the Secretary of War, together with the opinion of the Attorney-General, and it was determined that the conspirators should be tried by a military tribunal. It was desired, because of the state of public feeling, to have the matter over as early as possible.

The punishment of Booth was taken out of the hands of the law when he was shot. The trial of the others took place immediately. From the first there was no doubt of the guilt of Payne, who had attempted to murder Mr. Seward, the Secretary of State; of Herold, who failed to kill Mr. Johnson only through fear or lack of opportunity; or of Atzerodt, who was to have aided Herold. But there was doubt as to the degree of guilt of Mrs. Surratt. To this day there are those who consider her guiltless of the worst. The haste with which it was felt necessary to conduct the affair may have prevented full justice being done her. However that may have been, the fact that it was a woman who was condemned to die made a large faction view her hanging with the greatest repugnance. There was a great deal of feeling on both sides.

On the morning of the day on which the execution was to take place, the daughter of the condemned woman. Miss Annie Surratt, attempted to see the President to make a personal appeal for her mother. When she arrived, she was met by Secretary Seward, who was coming out of the President's office. He told her that it was useless for her to see the President; nothing could be done for her. The President had given orders that no one was to be admitted. When Miss Surratt was quite convinced of the hopelessness of any further attempt, she went home. The poor girl's grief was pitiful. Herold's two sisters also came fruitlessly to the White House to plead for their brother.

Because of the false light in which the President stood, a great deal of criticism grew out of these circumstances. He was blamed because he did not pardon Mrs. Surratt, or have the verdict commuted to imprisonment for life. He was blamed more when it was learned that there had been a recommenddation to mercy among the papers submitted to him by the court. The fact is, that Secretary Stanton, when he sent the papers to the President, kept back the note; Mr. Johnson did not know of it until afterward. When he did know of it, and of the fact that he was being blamed for not having interfered in the execution of Mrs. Surratt, he made a statement of his ignorance of the letter. Of course, very few of those who had been condemning him ever heard the denial. The incident increased the President's unpopularity. I believe that, had he seen the judge's recommendation to mercy, he would have been only too glad to save the woman. It is difficult to understand Mr. Stanton's motive in the matter.

Even his refusal to give an interview to Miss Surratt and the Herold girls was the source of scandal. It was reported by the President's enemies that he was intoxicated on the day they called. This was absolutely false. I denied the story indignantly at the time, but a denial does very little good when a slander has started on its way. The President was hard at work all day, closeted most of the time with Secretary Seward. He had taken every means to understand the case. The records show his conscientious desire to investigate. He had come to the conclusion that he could not interfere. Therefore, he did not think it wise to have an unnecessary and painful interview.

In all my experience there never has been an administration, unless it be the later one of Mr. Cleveland, where there has been such complete misunderstanding between the mass of the people and the executive as in that of Andrew Johnson. In my recollection it stands out as a feverish time, when events occurred without reason, without sequence, and larger than life. The war had been a time of great emotions—of suffering, heroism, and the many virtues of hardihood and tenderness that war brings out. Afterward the reverse side was the one in evidence. The spectacle of sudden loss and sudden elevation to wealth and prominence was equally demoralizing to the mass of those fitted to do nothing but plod. One result of all this was that at Washington we saw everywhere a very fury for office-holding, an egotistical thrusting of small men into the affairs of state, avalanches of advice and blame, equally stupid, from men without the slightest claim to be heard, but accustomed, during the years of the war, to consider national affairs their own.

Only the President and his secretaries know how many thousands of requests for favors came from women. They seemed to regard Mr. Johnson as their appointed guardian. It is probable that there was some reason for the confidence with which these feminine ambassadors made their wishes known, Mr.-

Johnson had an amiable weakness for women, particularly for pretty women. Those of us who were on duty in corridors and in anterooms saw many evidences of this fact. It seemed to be a purely unconscious tendency. He found it hard to believe that anything but merit and need could lurk behind a pair of beseeching woman's eyes.

The masculine specialty of the time was the crank. Every administration has them, of course, but they were particularly active during Mr. Johnson's administration. We learned how to handle them—^with gloves, but effectually. One man named Grapevine I remember very distinctly. He came to see the President several times. Finally, one day, when he was told that the President would not see him, he became furious. He raved like a madman, and threatened to kill Mr. Johnson. He said:

"What are you all doing here? I am the President, and that man is an impostor." Then he tried to force his way in to the President. At that stage, of course, I took him in hand and put him under arrest. When he was examined, it was discovered that he was armed with a large bowie-knife. He was sent to the insane asylum.

Another day a brother of a Union general came to the White House. He said his business was of great importance; it could not be postponed. It was impossible for the President to see him at that time, and the man became very angry. We talked to him, and thought we had persuaded him to go away and try again another time. I saw that he was not quite sane, so I walked quietly down-stairs with him and down the walk that led to the Treasury Department. About fifty paces from the White House I left him, thinking he would make no further trouble. As I turned my back, one of the doorkeepers called out:

"Look out! He is going to shoot you!" I turned, and saw him struggling with a soldier who happened to be passing just in time to knock up his arm as he aimed a pistol at me. There can be no doubt that, since he was armed with a perfectly new pistol, and since he tried to shoot the man who kept him from the President, he had intended to shoot Mr. Johnson. Episodes of that kind were of frequent occurrence in the White House. We dealt with them quietly, and they rarely got into the newspapers. It is usually a simple thing to manage cranks of both sexes. I have often had men and women refuse to leave the anteroom when they were told they could not see the President. When it was a lady who was persistent—

"All right," I would say; "make yourself perfectly comfortable, madam. Try this chair." After the lady had waited long enough to be thoroughly tired and the President had left his office by another door, I would inform her that the President had left his office for that day and invite her to return tomorrow. They rarely came back, and there was never any disturbance.

It is perhaps not surprising that there should have begun, just at this time, an epidemic of dishonesty among those who wanted to make money out of the government, to be matched, if the furore of disclosures and investigations through which we are now passing is any evidence, only by the one just ended. Then, however, it was the petty office-holders and a host of unprincipled hangers-on. The peculiar opportunities for easily made money offered by the times were a great temptation.

Before Mr. Johnson had been in office many months, it was discovered that a doorkeeper who stood at the entrance to the President's office had been charging an admission fee to those who wanted to approach the President with any of the thousands of requests that were made to him. The man had amassed a comfortable little competence before the fact was discovered and he was removed.

On November 25, 1865, I resigned my position with the Metropolitan Police force to become the President's private policeman. From this time I was associated much more intimately with Mr. Johnson. I was with him almost as much as I was with President Lincoln when I accompanied him to City Point and Richmond. Virtually every day that Mr. Johnson went out driving I went with him. Sometimes I rode by the side of the carriage on a saddle-horse which had been bought for Colonel Robert Johnson, but which he never rode. More often I sat by th^ President's side.

The work of the executive office was complicated and unending. The President needed all of the long hours he spent at his desk. Sometimes, among all the difficulties presented to him to solve, a humorous episode occurred which freshened the atmosphere.

JOHNSON IN THE WHITE HOUSE

After a while it would filter out to us who stood in corridors and anterooms. A man whose name was Gordon, I think, was very much exercised. He was in a panic because the negroes who were then the charges of the Freedmen's Bureau in his district were dying fast. At that rate he figured that in about eight months the entire negro population would perish. He wanted the President to do something about it. A Southern woman who did not like the provisional governor in her State, and who was evidently a consumer of romance, suggested that the President should come there in disguise and investigate for himself. Then there was one girl—a very young girl—who wanted a rest of several months to be given to her sweetheart in the army. She said he was "all tired out." She reminded the President that he had told her that their attachment ought to be tried, and said that he must acknowledge that it had been.

VI

DISSENSION WITH THE RADICALS

WHILE Mr. Johnson was amused over these incidents, he talked little about passing events; in fact, he talked little about anything. I never saw a man who was more content to hold his own counsel. One thing was evident, however: the President was changing his mind about the Southern people. He had been so very bitter in regard to the rebellion, and apparently antagonistic to Mr. Lincoln's sympathetic tolerance, that every one expected severity in his measures toward the South. We now feel sure that Secretary Seward, who had been at one with President Lincoln, influenced President Johnson in those early days.

No one knows what were the rigors of Mr. Seward's position throughout this administration, standing between a vehement President and a vehement Congress, and attempting to influence each faction to readjust and modify its views. With Charles Sumner, Thaddeus Stevens, and men of their stamp, he failed utterly. As had been the case all through Mr. Lincoln's administration, they refused to modify their radical principles. With the President he did not succeed completely. Could the world know of the fruitless and painful interviews which Secretary Seward had with these men, and then observe the spectacle of his steadfast loyalty to the President, of whose conduct he often disapproved, no man would emerge from the contentions of this period with more honor in the estimation of his countrymen. This, however, is to anticipate the contention in which Mr. Johnson, yielding to what he believed to be Mr. Lincoln's policy toward the defeated South, and influenced by his own comprehension of conditions in the Confederate States, was moved to lay aside his own animosity toward the greater part of the Southern leaders. Toward some of them—those whom he considered responsible for leading their region into rebellion—he never softened.

The truth is that Mr. Johnson was not moved very much in his estimate of men by the way in which they had treated him personally. If they had failed in what he considered their public duty, he could be severe enough; but, except in two cases, I believe he felt no personal enmity to them. Of "Parson" Brownlow, his bitterest enemy in his own State, I heard Mr. Johnson speak most pleasantly. This is all the more remarkable when we remember that, having left nothing undone to defeat the President's wishes with regard to Tennessee, Brownlow telegraphed to Congress the news of the ratification of the Fourteenth Amendment with the insulting message, "Tell this to the dead dog of the White House!" In his public addresses he inveighed against Sumner and Stevens and Wendell Phillips, but when he met them he seemed wholly unprejudiced. One of his bitterest political enemies related that on the day following the vote on impeachment, when he had voted to impeach, he met Andrew Johnson, who smiled and held out his hand. In the same manner, in spite of his fierceness toward the rebellion, he was now made to believe in the loyalty of the South.

One thing that specially moved Mr. Johnson to this latter belief was the optimistic report made by General Grant after a tour through the heart of the Confederacy. He stated that he saw everywhere an intention to return to full allegiance to the Union as soon as the conditions of that return were established. When the report was sent to Congress, where it was pointedly ignored, Senator Sumner pronounced it a whitewashing message.

These are some of the motives that influenced the President's message to Congress when it assembled in December, 1865. I remember how great was the surprise at the tenor of the message, and how general the admiration of the dignity and clearness with which it was expressed. In the newspapers and in the conversation of men there was scarcely a dissenting voice; the President at once took a position as statesman which he had never occupied before. Men like George Bancroft cordially endorsed his attitude. The South felt that a champion had arisen. The only dissenting voice was from the extreme Northern element in Congress—the Radicals, as they were called.

While any discussion of President Johnson's public acts does not come strictly within the limits of my-

DISSENSION WITH THE RADICALS

field of personal reminiscence, I feel that it is necessary to touch upon some features of the President's long contention with Congress.

I believe firmly that President Johnson wished to carry out the policy which had been advocated by Mr. Lincoln before he died. I believe, moreover, that it was substantially the policy which President Lincoln would have attempted to carry through if he had lived. There is, however, this one point of difference: meeting the fierce opposition which the Radical element in Congress displayed. President Lincoln, who knew how to manage men and to compromise, would have yielded in minor points, where he could have done so and still carry out his policy of immediate and practical help for the South. It was in this one feature that President Johnson failed to meet the requirements of his position.

In President Lincoln's last speech he expressed, so far as he had been able to see his way, his plan of reconstruction. There should be a general amnesty, with a few exceptions. For the rest, when the South had banished slavery, it should be allowed to reorganize its State governments under the "Louisiana plan." The Louisiana plan was to allow the loyal minority in each State to form a government. Congress would recognize any republican form of government which should be established by insurgents who should have taken the amnesty oath and were regularly qualified voters in 1860, provided the votes cast were not less than one-tenth in number of the votes cast that year. This plan of reconstruction rested upon the theory that the Southern States, having no right under the Constitution to withdraw from the Union, were still members of the Union. While rebels were present in each State, the loyal minority were still citizens of the United States, and had a right to representation in Congress.

Now, the war having been fought by the Federal authority upon just this principle, that the Southern States had no right to withdraw from the Union, President Lincoln's plan was merely the logical consequence of the theory. It presented difficulties and inconsistencies, no doubt, and it was hard to conceive seriously of States which, during the war, had been at the same time in and out of the Union; but, then, there was not a single theory prevalent at the time which did not present inconsistencies. Those who, with Thaddeus Stevens, had been most fierce in declaring that the Southern States had no constitutional right to secede, were most vehement, when the war was over, in maintaining that the Confederacy was a conquered power beyond the pale of consideration from good Republicans, and not to be restored to the Union until she had been soundly punished for her sins. The abolitionists, who, with Charles Sumner, were most vehement in advocating the equal rights of man, were determined to foist upon the Southern States, without their consent, the franchise for the lately emancipated slaves, and to disfranchise the ruling element.

In his eagerly expected message President Johnson expressed the principle which had animated

DISSENSION WITH THE RADICALS

President Lincoln: the Southern States were still in the Union, their functions had been suspended, not destroyed. The Thirteenth Amendment, which abolished slavery, having been passed, and the amnesty oath having been taken, the next step was for their representatives to resume their seats in Congress. Congress alone had the right to determine on the eligibility of members. The question of negro suffrage was to be left to the States, as had been the matter of suffrage from the beginning. Before Congress had met, and pending their action, Mr. Johnson had begun the work of restoring the governments of those States which were ready to convene loyal assemblies, after the plan followed in Louisiana. There had been some dissension in the cabinet over the matter. Under the influence of the extreme Radicals, Secretary Stanton had endeavored to introduce a requirement as to negro suffrage, while Speed and Harlan were in opposition. The latter two soon withdrew, as was proper in the circumstances, while Stanton, apparently restored to sympathy, remained in office.

From the principles laid down in his message President Johnson never swerved. Every act passed by Congress that violated these principles he consistently vetoed. That the Freedmen's Bureau Act and the Civil Rights Act would receive his condemnation was a foregone conclusion. From the comments of the press throughout the country there was no doubt that the mass of the people were with the President.

With the veto of the Freedmen's Bureau Act, which made no uncertain declaration of the President's intentions, began a most amazing chapter in the history of our Congress. Since a struggle was imminent, it was necessary to be sure of a two-thirds Republican majority in order to pass acts over the veto. Every expedient was resorted to: a senator was rejected on a re-examination of credentials, before approved; a would-be honorable senator was forced to break his pair; in order that another pair might not be broken, a dying man was hurried to the Senate, only to find that the vote had been taken in haste to exclude his. It was by such means that the bill was passed over the veto. But the majority was too small. It was proposed to admit two States, below the requirement of numbers, on an abolition platform dictated by the Radicals, in order to swell the number. One such State was actually admitted. An examination of the speeches in both House and Senate of those months shows them filled with a wild alarm, not for the country, but for the Republican party.

"We need their votes," said Charles Sumner, of the negroes.

"If the Southern States are readmitted on equal terms, what of our majority?" was on every Radical tongue.

It is necessary to observe, moreover, that this opposition to any but the most radical and severe measures toward the South did not result from the action of President Johnson. Before the President's message had been sent to Congress the opposition had been thoroughly organized; the principle had been laid down that only Congress should preside over re-

DISSENSION WITH THE RADICALS

construction. It had, moreover, earlier than this been organized and powerful enough to oppose President Lincoln most bitterly in his efforts to restore the South without punitive measures. It had been in abeyance for a short time because the triumphant end of the war had made Mr. Lincoln virtually a dictator. But his death saved Abraham Lincoln from the bitterest struggle of his life.

Mr. Ward Lamon, who was one of the most intimate of Mr. Lincoln's friends, evidently believed this. He said to Mr. Johnson (the letter can be produced):

> I had many and free conversations with him [Lincoln] on this very subject of reconstruction. I was made entirely certain by his own repeated declarations to me that he would exert all his authority to bring about an immediate and perfect reconciliation between the two sections of the country. As far as depended upon him, he would have had the Southern States represented in both houses of Congress within the shortest possible time.... He knew the base designs of the Radicals to keep up the strife for their own advantage. There can be no doubt that the Northern Disunionists would now be as loud in their denunciation of his policy as they are of yours.... If there be any insult upon his reputation which we should resent more than another, it is the assertion that he would have been a tool and an instrument in the hands of such men as those who now lead the heartless and unprincipled contest against you.

At the time that all these things were happening we saw at the White House no evidence that they affected the President in any personal way. He was such a reticent man that I was surprised at a speech he made on the 22d of February, 1866. A great crowd had assembled in the White House grounds. They wanted a speech. By reason of his unexpected championship of the Southern States, President Johnson had become a figure in the public eye. He began to speak to the crowd calmly and dispassionately. He spoke of the question at issue before the country. He said that there had been two extreme elements in the national life—that of the South, which, having asserted itself for slavery, had been suppressed; that of the North, which, now beginning to show itself, was just as intolerant. For himself he belonged to neither class. He was for the Union slavery or no slavery. The "conscious intelligent traitors" should be punished; there should be amnesty for the multitude. . . . To admit that a State was out of the Union was the very thing the nation had been fighting against, insisting that this was something a State could not do.

The crowd became enthusiastic; the President began to speak more warmly. I know he must have been sore because of the revenge which Congress had taken for his veto of the Freedmen's Bureau Act. For they had retaliated by refusing to admit the representatives of his own State, of whose record he was so proud and which he had done so much to keep loyal. He said that Congress was governed by "an irresponsible central directory" which did not represent the people—was no Congress. Some one in the crowd shouted,

"Name them!"

The President hesitated a moment; then he said,

DISSENSION WITH THE RADICALS

"Yes, I will name them"—at this there was great excitement—"Thaddeus Stevens, Charles Sumner."

From this time on there was a great change in the way people regarded him. One man said to him,

"Your speech made me feel mortified." And I think this would express the feeling that most of Andrew Johnson's friends had about this most unfortunate matter. Still, he showed no feeling, but went on with the programme he had made for himself. On the 18th of April a delegation of sailors and soldiers came to see him. He spoke to them in much the same tone as that of his speech of the 2 2d of February. He assured them of his unalterable determination to "stick to his position." He spoke contemptuously of men who, when he was battling for the Union in the Senate and in his own State, were "lolling in ease and comfort. . . ." Now they were attacking him, ". . . the whole pack, Tray, Blanche, and Sweetheart, little dogs and all, snapping at my heels." I suppose this was very undignified and bad policy, but the crowd enjoyed it, and nothing could have been a better description of the attacks made upon the President by certain men in Congress.

There is one thing which must be understood. These addresses of the President seemed much more undignified to the country at large than to those who heard them. In the first place, the newspaper man, then as now, was on the outlook for a sensation. In fact, there was less regard for the truth then, even with the better class of journals, than there is to-day.

8

Party feeling and interests ran high, and editors were violently partisan.

More than this, Mr. Johnson's manner in delivering public speeches was one which could not be translated into newspaper language. I realized this when I stood near him on the portico while he talked to the soldiers and sailors. He had a calm, assured way of talking which gave the most startling remarks authority. His bearing was quiet and dignified, his voice low and sympathetic. He had one of the best voices for public speaking that I have ever heard. It was singularly penetrating; he could make it carry to the edge of the largest gathering without effort. Yet it was always a pleasant voice. I have been startled myself to read the same speech in the paper that I had heard the day before. One would think, from what was written, that a violent demagogue was brandishing his arms and shrieking at the top of his lungs. Mr. Johnson was an orator; half of what was said was in the personal relation between the audience and himself, and, being an orator, he was often swayed by the emotion of the crowd. Had he been sympathetically reported, the country would have had a different impression of him.

There is a story I have heard which illustrates both this magnetic quality of the man and his fearlessness. It was in the early days of the struggle in Tennessee, when he was hated by the whole secession element. He was to address a meeting in the tov/n-hall. He had been informed on good authority that half a dozen men were ready to shoot him as soon as he

DISSENSION WITH THE RADICALS

appeared before the audience. When he appeared on the platform, he advanced to the speaker's stand. Something held the crowd to silence while he deliberately pulled a pistol out of his pocket. He laid it on the table while a spell-bound crowd hung on his movements. Then at last he spoke:

"I understand," he said, in his placid way, "that the first business before the meeting is to shoot me. I move that the meeting proceed to business." During the few minutes that he scanned the audience there was breathless silence. At last, when no one moved, he began his address in rather a disappointed manner.

Except when the excitement of a crowd stirred him to intemperance of language, the President possessed the dignity of reticence.

As the summer came on, my drive with Mr. Johnson became a daily occurrence, and often lasted the greater part of the afternoon. We often took the children with us, and had a picnic. I think the greatest source of recreation the President had was in his grandchildren. His own youngest son was about thirteen at this time and had his own pursuits; but the grandchildren were always ready.

With a carriage full of children we would drive to some place by Rock Creek, Pierce's Mill, or elsewhere. There was one retired little meadow by the stream of which we were all fond. There the children would fish, wade, or pick flowers, and the President would watch them and reflect. We would drive home with the carriage filled with flowers.

When we were alone we always stopped at some quiet and beautiful spot, where Mr. Johnson could walk for an hour or more, almost always in silence. He often went to Glenwood Cemetery. There was something in the peace of such a place that appealed to him. One day he had been wandering about in Glenwood reading the inscriptions on the tombstones when I heard him laughing. I went up to him. He did not laugh very often.

"Look there, Crook," he said, pointing to two graves side by side. On the first was," Sacred to the Memory of my Wife—By her disconsolate husband." The other grave, dated two years later, was that of the second wife.

"It didn't take that fellow long to get over his first affliction, did it?" said the President.

I fully believe that, had the elections occurred immediately after the adjournment of Congress in the summer of 1866, the Radicals would have been defeated. It was not that the President had not made many enemies by his unwise speech on the 22d of February. It was because, even in New England, there was a general distrust of the Radical programme. In April, Harper's Weekly and The Nation had commented on the weak points of the leadership of Thad Stevens. There was a strong sentiment against further punishment of the South. There was much doubt as to the wisdom of negro suffrage. All of the efforts of the Radicals during the summer— Wendell Phillips making campaign speeches every-where and proposing to impeach the President, Ben Butler touring the country denouncing the President

DISSENSION WITH THE RADICALS

Sumner instructing large audiences in Massachusetts —would probably have been fruitless had Mr. Johnson himself not made his second great mistake.

As I have said before, the President was accustomed in making public speeches to come into personal relations with his audiences. In his career in Tennessee this method had been largely a factor in his success. Now, in his anxiety over the great questions at stake—the issue to be determined by the fall elections—he determined to make a direct appeal to the voters. There was to be a great ceremony at the unveiling of the Douglas monument at Chicago. Mr. Johnson made attendance on this the occasion for a partial tour of the country. Philadelphia, New York, Albany, Cleveland, St. Louis, and Chicago were to be visited. Secretaries Welles and Randall, with Secretary Seward, General Grant, and Admiral Farragut, were of the party.

Mr. Johnson had an unfortunate propensity for coining phrases which could be used to ridicule him. On one occasion he had referred to himself as the Moses who offered himself to lead the country out of bondage. He figured as "Moses" in street songs for months. On another occasion he had talked of "swinging round the circle" of political conviction from North to South. This projected trip was immediately labelled "swinging round the circle," and the newspaper men of the country took out their writing-pads prepared to have a thoroughly enjoyable time.

The President had always been a popular figure with newspaper correspondents. Whether he was to be admired or blamed, he was always an energetic and vivid personality. There was sure to be something to report. Again, the journals at that time were yellow beyond possibility of emulation by the papers of to-day. The following is a specimen of the type in many of the news-sheets throughout the country: "Andy, Andy, you are terribly popular with the rabble! Everything that smells, but does not perfume; everything rotten and mouldering, whatever is corrupt and putrefying, sticks to thee! Toads and owls howl to thee! Jackals and hyenas snuffle after thee. . . ." There were newspaper correspondents accompanying the party, but, as will be seen later, they were entirely unable to stem the tide of sensationalism. The tour was immediately pronounced an undignified departure from the custom of former presidents. The unfortunate reputation for drunkenness which had fastened upon Mr. Johnson was made to do duty again, with rumors of immense stores of liquors which made the special cars travelling bar-rooms. The country prepared to be shocked.

The country was disappointed in the earlier stages of the journey. There was a moderate amount of enthusiasm in the reception of the party in Philadelphia and New York. In Albany the atmosphere was chilling; in Auburn there was a remarkable speech against the Republican Party from Ex-President Fillmore. At Cleveland the crowd was disorderly. The President was interrupted again and again; there was evidently an organized movement to prevent his speaking. He attempted to reply to insulting interruptions, lost his temper, was baited by the crowd, and for a time all semblance of dignity was lost. Ultimately he pulled himself together, silenced his tormentors, and closed triumphantly. At Chicago there was the same disorderly crowd, and undoubtedly preconcerted interruptions. The President was provoked into intemperance and a declaration that he would "kick the Radicals out." These unfortunate scenes were immediately telegraphed over the country, with every embellishment possible. They lost the President the elections; gave the Radicals an overwhelming majority; made possible the horrors of congressional reconstruction.

After this there was no possibility of stemming the tide of unpopularity. The President figured in the popular mind as almost a monster. The Atlantic *Monthly*, which had always stood for all that was most conservative and careful in the country, published a series of studies, advertised widely by the magazine as " Remarkable articles on President Johnson," in which Mr. Johnson was studied as though he were some abnormal product of an alien race. His traits are analyzed thus:

> . . . his gross inconsistencies of opinion and policy, his shameless betrayal of party, incapacity to hold himself to his word, his hatred of a cause the moment its defenders cease to flatter him. *his habit of administering laws he has vetoed* on the principle that they do not mean what he vetoed them for meaning, his delight in little tricks of low cunning. . . . It would seem that, in dealing with such a man as Andrew Johnson, it is the part of wisdom to suspect the worst, . . . a spiteful, inflated, and unprincipled egotist.

VII

THE IMPEACHMENT

I WATCHED him after he returned from this disastrous trip, when he was the most unpopular man in the country, and threats of impeachment were a matter of daily occurrence. His manner was absolutely as when he first took upon himself the cares of office. In our daily drives there was never a reference to what was passing. He spoke, when he spoke at all, about indifferent things. There was not an added line in his face. And yet there was evidence, from that time on, that he had learned his lesson; that, as he once said to me, when he was convinced that he had been wrong, he was ready to change. For never after this, so far as I remember, was he betrayed by the warmth of his feeling into an unwise public utterance. During the whole of the impeachment trial, when the temptation to appeal from his enemies to the "plain people" on whose final judgment he relied must have been almost overpowering, he refrained altogether from public speaking. His habit of bandying words with the mob was overcome.

The legislators came back to the second half of the Thirty - ninth Congress elated over their victory at the polls, and convinced that it was in their power to

THE IMPEACHMENT

carry their whole reconstruction programme. There was the greatest dissatisfaction expressed with the constitutions of the Southern States, now largely reorganized. The new governments had passed repressive measures against the negroes. The Abolitionists considered that these measures virtually re-enslaved the emancipated.

An incident which the Radicals seized upon as an evidence of the absolute failure of the President's reconstruction policy was an unfortunate riot over elections in New Orleans. He was accused of not having responded to the call of the governor for Federal aid. Again the President explained that the telegram of the governor had been withheld from him by Secretary Stanton. And again the country heard the charge, and not the refutation. And again it is hard to understand Secretary Stanton's action in this matter.

The activities of Congress of the winter and spring of 1866-67 were in two directions. A series of acts embodying the congressional theories of reconstruction was passed and a long investigation of the President's conduct was undertaken with a view to discovering grounds for impeachment. The first was tragic, culminating as it did in negro suffrage, the disfranchisement of the majority of the better class of Southerners, the dominion of carpet-baggers, terror and suffering for eleven States. The second was pure comedy, exhibiting the congressional species in farcical specialties. In their reconstruction acts Congress worsted the President, depriving him of control over the eleven

Southern States, over the army, and at last, by the Tenure of Office Act, over his own cabinet. In their attempts to prove him worthy of impeachment, the President's record worsted Congress, Even the two Houses, full of enemies, could find no blot in it.

As fast as the reconstruction measures were passed, Mr. Johnson executed them. He held, with the Constitution, that his control over legislation ended with his veto. With relation to the matter of negro suffrage, Mr. Johnson's attitude was fully expressed in an interview which had taken place the year before. A deputation of leading negroes, headed by Frederick Douglass, called upon the President to plead for their right to the suffrage. Mr. Johnson's manner to them was quiet, even gentle. It was interesting to see how deftly he prevented the interview from becoming a discussion and utilized it to state his own position. He suggested emigration to them. He asserted that each community was better prepared to settle questions of suffrage than was Congress. He said that he opposed negro suffrage on the ground that, carried out, it would inevitably lead to a race war. He ended, "God knows I have no desire but the welfare of the whole human race."

With regard to the impeachment investigation, there had been, since the President's veto of the first Freedmen's Bureau Act, a continual rumble of threats of impeachment in both houses of Congress. At last, in January, 1867, Mr. Ashley, of Ohio, one of Mr. Johnson's most bitter enemies, introduced a resolution to investigate the course of the President with

THE IMPEACHMENT

a view to impeachment. The Judiciary Committee was empowered to conduct the investigation, to summon witnesses, and to sit during the summer recess if necessary.

Throughout the investigation the President was calm and untroubled. When a bank employee went with embarrassment to inform him that his accounts were demanded, he laughed.

"Let them have them, if they want them. All of my business affairs are open to the world. I have nothing to be ashamed of."

It must not be considered that either the proceedings of the Judiciary Committee or the severity of congressional reconstruction was approved by the country at large. Mr. Ashley's virulence was so great that he had been reproved by the Speaker of the House, Many Radical newspapers throughout the nation disapproved of the measures passed by Congress. Even Senator Wilson, Charles Sumner's colleague from Massachusetts, who had been most vehement in his pleadings for the "poor, lowly, downtrodden freedmen," said of the white men on his return from a tour of the Southern States:

"For myself, I want no more punishments than have already been inflicted on these men. They have suffered and have been disappointed more than any body of men in the history of the world."

It seems hard to understand the hysteria which swept over both houses of Congress during these abnormal years. It has been very generally stated that the opposition aroused by the President's stubborn resistance to congressional control was responsible for it, that each antagonist pushed the other into extremes. In one case this is undoubtedly true. The measures passed by Congress at the end of the struggle could not have been possible at the beginning. It was not that they were new, but that the President's action had aroused so much opposition that the element which had advocated these measures from the beginning came into control. The significant fact is that, while, on the part of the President, the contest goaded him into unwise public utterances, his policy was not altered by the bitterness of his feeling in one particular. The principles expressed in the first message, so generally applauded by the country at the time, were the same that dictated the last protest to Congress when he had failed to prevent the intemperate legislation that had disgraced it. The fault, if it were a fault, lay not in his having been hurried into inconsidered action, but in his not having compromised, at the beginning of the controversy, where he might have done so, with a yielding of theory, but not of practical kindliness, toward the South.

The long-brewing contention with Secretary Stanton came to a head during the summer of 1867. Mr. Stanton's career in Mr. Johnson's cabinet had been a curious one. It was generally known that, during Mr. Lincoln's administration, Mr. Stanton had frequently assumed that he alone was responsible for the maintenance of the Government. Mr. Lincoln, who knew how to utilize every element that was presented to him, and was entirely without personal feeling, had very little difficulty in managing Stanton. He knew how to make use of his Secretary's undoubted patriotism, his force, his earnestness; he knew how to harness his unruly temper. Lincoln was impervious to offence because of his humorous acceptance of conditions.

Mr. Johnson was not skilful in managing men—men whom he could not influence. From the first Mr. Stanton was an element of discord. A number of the Radicals had influenced him to introduce a negro-suffrage clause into the first reconstruction measures discussed by the cabinet. His natural harshness of nature led him to desire a severe policy toward the South. And yet, when it became apparent that the President and three members of the cabinet were in favor of carrying out the policy of Mr. Lincoln, he apparently acquiesced. At all events, he remained in the cabinet, while the other members who were in opposition resigned. Each of the President's messages, each of the vetoes, Stanton apparently approved. He was so strong in pronouncing the Tenure of Office Act unconstitutional that he was asked to write the message accompanying the veto. He pleaded some indisposition, however, and avoided doing it.

The constant friction over the administration of the War Department became unbearable. Two instances have been already given where Mr. Stanton had withheld information from the President which he should have had—the note for mercy in the case of Mrs. Surratt and the telegram of the Governor of New Orleans asking for Federal aid. In both of these cases Mr. Johnson's position before the country had been very much injured by the Secretary's action. What was left to the President of executive powers over the Southern States was nullified by Mr. Stanton's disposition to balk him at every turn. There can be no doubt that Mr. Stanton was sincere in his idea that it was necessary, in order to prevent the country from disintegration, that he remain in Mr. Johnson's cabinet. This delusion, fostered by years of autocratic power over his own department, was responsible for the lack of taste in Mr. Stanton's remaining in the cabinet of a man whose enemy he was. It is another example of the lack of balance in the public life of the period.

The President had borne this irritating defiance with what was, in a man of his type, remarkable patience.

In August, 1867, the President suspended Secretary Stanton from office, appointing General Grant in his place. It was during the recess of Congress. Under the Tenure of Office Act he had the right to suspend a member of his cabinet during the recess of Congress, so he was strictly within his rights. The contest would come later, when the removal was reported to Congress for approval. Mr. Stanton had no course but to yield, and General Grant performed the duties of the office. Up to this point there had been, on the whole, pleasant relations between Mr. Johnson and General Grant. Grant was the popular idol; his friendship was an important item.

It was in the same summer that the President and

THE IMPEACHMENT

I were on our way home one evening in what is now Rock Creek Park. A summer storm came up, and it began to rain in torrents. We were well outside the limits of the present city when we came upon a poor woman struggling along the road. She had a heavy baby in her arms, and her shabby clothes were already soaked through with the rain. Mr. Johnson ordered the driver to stop and take her in. She climbed up, trying not to soil the cushions with her dripping clothes. The President sat opposite her, when the carriage was rolling on again, saying nothing, as was his habit, but looking at the mother and baby with very kind eyes. She lived on what is now Florida Avenue—which we then called Boundary Street, between Fourteenth and Fifteenth Streets. When we stopped opposite her little two-story frame house, Mr. Johnson got out and helped her out and up the steps. She never knew that it was the President who had taken her home. When we got back to the White House, Mr. Johnson told Slade, the steward, to give the driver a hot toddy. He had been sitting on the box through all the storm, and did not have his oilskins to protect him. Mr. Johnson, although he never seemed to be taking much notice of what was going on about him, always saw things like that.

Congress convened on September i, 1867. Every one awaited its action with a good deal of excitement, for it was generally understood that when the President submitted the question of the removal of Secretary Stanton from the War Department the final struggle between Congress and Mr. Johnson would begin. It was a foregone conclusion that the President's action would not be endorsed. It was, with those of us who knew the President, equally certain that he would persist in his determination not to allow Mr. Stanton to remain in his cabinet. Of course my sympathies were with Mr. Johnson. Even if I had not felt that Mr. Stanton was a harsh and arrogant man, I could not have failed to see how he had thwarted the President at every turn. One surely did not have to know about constitutional questions to understand that a president should be surrounded by a cabinet whose members are in sympathy with him, and that if one member consistently opposes him and all the other members, and refuses to resign, the President should have the right to dismiss him.

At this time particularly, when, since the Southern States had been again placed under military governors, the retention of Mr. Stanton as Secretary of War meant that Mr. Johnson could not have the slightest control over the administration of the unfortunate eleven States, it was necessary to remove Mr. Stanton. The President naturally desired to do the little that was left in his power to make their condition more bearable.

Within the time prescribed by the Tenure of Office Act, the President reported the removal of Secretary Stanton, with his reasons. On the 14th of January Congress refused to acquiesce, and ordered his restoration to office. At this point General Grant yielded his portfolio of office to Secretary Stanton and retired from the position. General Grant's action made

THE IMPEACHMENT

of President Johnson a bitter enemy. Together with Stanton he became the object of the President's hatred. In fact, General Grant seemed to stand, in Mr. Johnson's eyes, as the type of all the opposition the President had undergone. It is useless to discuss whether General Grant was right or wrong. He acted as he thought right. He was a modest man, and it was distasteful to him to seem to usurp a position claimed by another man. I believe that he was honestly convinced that, until the constitutionality of the removal of Secretary Stanton was decided, his was the proper course. But to President Johnson, General Grant's action was that of a traitor.

One week after the action of Congress the President removed Mr. Stanton and appointed General Lorenzo Thomas in his place. The struggle between Stanton and Thomas had a humorous side. General Thomas made a daily visit to the War Department to demand possession of the office and the records, and Secretary Stanton as regularly refused to yield his position. In order to prevent a night attack upon his fortress, Stanton had a bed in his private office.

On the 21st General Thomas called and made his demand. There was parleying, but Secretary Stanton reserved his decision. On the 22d, early in the morning, by the orders of Secretary Stanton, General Thomas was arrested. He was taken to the stationhouse, but was immediately released on bail. This was done with the intention of having a court verdict on the matter. General Thomas then repaired to the office of the Secretary of War, and made his second demand. Mr. Stanton refused to yield, and General Thomas refused to depart.

Immediately after this the Secretary of War *ad interim* was tried and released. He continued to attend cabinet meetings and to make demands upon the Secretary of War. He became generally known as "Ad Interim Thomas."

On the third day after the removal of Secretary Stanton the House of Representatives decided that "the President be impeached" before the Senate "for high crimes and misdemeanors."

The managers of the prosecution were John A. Bingham, George S. Boutwell, James F. Wilson, Thomas Williams, Benjamin F. Butler, John A. Logan, and Thaddeus Stevens. The most bitter against the President were Butler, Stevens, and Wilson. Butler opened the prosecution. There were eleven articles of impeachment, but the only actual charge—^that of having disregarded the Tenure of Office Act in the removal of Stanton—was contained in the eleventh.

All over the country men wished to take a part in choosing the President's counsel. Suggestions poured in, and people flocked to the White House, each one with a candidate to put forward. Country lawyers sent in briefs, with the very evident hope that they might be chosen. Others, not so modest, directly offered their services. However much difference of opinion there might be as to other men, the country was virtually unanimous in putting forward the claim of Benjamin R. Curtis, who needed no advocacy, for

THE IMPEACHMENT

the President appointed him immediately. The other members of the counsel were William M. Evarts, Thomas A. R. Nelson, and Judge Jeremiah S. Black. Judge Black had hardly agreed to undertake the case before he resigned. This occasioned a great deal of discussion. It was said that Judge Black had given up the case because of its hopelessness, and this gossip injured Mr. Johnson's cause. That the President did not announce the real reason was to his credit.

The true story of the transaction is this: Judge Black was one of the attorneys for the Vela Alta claim. Vela Alta was an island near San Domingo which was rich in guano. The President was asked to interfere in the contest as to its possession by pronouncing it the property of a United States company. Whether the contention was a just one or not it is, of course, impossible to discuss here. Secretary Seward was opposed to United States interference. But the unfortunate thing was that just at this time Judge Black pressed the case, sending in as endorsers four out of the seven managers of the case against the President, Mr. Butler among them. The inference that Mr. Johnson's consent to act as these gentlemen desired might possibly influence their attitude toward the President is an obvious one. It was obvious enough to cause Mr. Johnson to refuse to interfere. Thereupon Judge Black promptly resigned from the counsel, feeling, in all probability, that his participation in the trial would prevent success of the private enterprise. William S. Groesbeck was appointed in his place.

Another matter for debate was whether Senator

Wade, who was acting-President of the Senate since Mr. Johnson had become President, should have a vote. In the event of the President's being convicted of the charge against him, Mr. Wade would of course become President. It would seem hardly decorous for him to cast a vote; but it was decided, after much discussion, that his vote should count. Mr. Wade was jubilant. In fact, it was stated that he had already selected his cabinet. I happened to be present when Mr. Johnson was told this. He chuckled, and said:

"Old Wade is counting his chickens before they are hatched."

The formal opening of the trial was on the 13th of March. The President's counsel asked for forty days in which to prepare the arguments. They were rather ungraciously refused, and were allowed ten days instead. The court then adjourned until the 23d.

During this preliminary time and during the trial, the spiritualists all over the country tried to gain a proselyte by playing upon the President's natural anxiety as to the outcome. A Mrs. Colby sent him marvellous messages from Lincoln and other statesmen. The messages were, like most of their kind, illiterate, impudent, and absurd. The "Davenport Brothers" also tried to gain his interest. It was even reported that President Johnson was a spiritualist. Although he was a member of no church, the President was as definite in his orthodox religious views as he was in his political policy. There was nothing of the mystic in his nature, and he was too clear-sighted for mere superstition.

THE IMPEACHMENT

On the 23d of March, when the actual trial began, the President took leave of three of his counsel—Mr. Evarts, Mr. Curtis, and Mr. Nelson—who had come to the White House for a final discussion. I was near them as they stood together in the portico. Mr. Johnson's manner was entirely calm and unconcerned. He shook hands with each of them in turn, and said:

"Gentlemen, my case is in your hands; I feel sure that you will protect my interests." Then he returned to his office. I went off with the gentlemen. By the desire of the President, I accompanied them to the Capitol every day.

When, from my seat in the gallery, I looked down on the Senate chamber, I had a moment of almost terror. It was not because of the great assemblage; it was rather in the thought that one could feel in the mind of every man and woman there that for the first time in the history of the United States a President was on trial for more than his life—his place in the judgment of his countrymen and of history.

There was a painful silence when the counsel for the President filed in and took their places. They were seated under the desk of the presiding officer—in this case. Chief-Justice Chase—on the right-hand side of the Senate chamber. The managers for the prosecution were already in their seats. Every seat in the gallery was occupied.

The dignity with which the proceedings opened served to heighten the sense of awe. It persevered during the routine business of reading the journal and while the President's reply was being read; but when Manager Butler arose to make the opening address for the prosecution, there was a change.

His speech was a violent attack upon the President. It was clever. Actually blameless incidents were made to seem traitorous. The address was so bitter, and yet so almost theatrical, that it seemed unreal. I wondered at the time why it so impressed me. In Butler's later action—to which I shall hereafter refer—came a possible explanation of this impression.

The trial lasted three weeks. The President, of course, never appeared. In that particular the proceedings lacked a spectacular interest they might have had. Every day the President had a consultation with his lawyers. For the rest, he attended to the routine work of his position. He was absolutely calm through it all. The very night of the 23d he gave a reception to as many of the members of Congress as would come. I was fully prepared to have the White House deserted, but, instead of that, it was crowded. I wondered why men who hated the President so bitterly could accept his hospitality until I came to a group of about fifteen Radicals gathered together in the East Room, where they had proceeded after paying their respects to the President. They were laughing together, and teasing one another like boys.

"What are you here for?" I heard.

"And you—what are you doing here yourself?"

"Why, I wanted to see how Andy takes it," was the answer. I thought to myself as I passed them that they were getting small satisfaction out of that, for no one could have seen the slightest difference in Mr. Johnson's manner. He greeted every one as pleasantly as though it were a surprise party come to congratulate him on his statesmanship.

It was the same with the affairs of his personal life. If he had any doubt as to the outcome of the trial, he did not allow it to affect his interest in those who had any claim on him. It was in the midst of the excitement following the impeachment that Slade, the steward, fell ill. Slade was a mulatto, a very intelligent man, and the President had a great deal of confidence in him. I remember very well when, on the 2d of March, I went with Mr. Johnson to see Slade in his home.

The poor fellow was suffering when we entered. He had asthma, and it was pitiful to hear him struggle for breath. Mr. Johnson went up to the bed, and took the sick man's hand in his.

"How are you to-day, Slade?" he asked, kindly, and when the dying man shook his head, the President tried to cheer him up.

Slade's death followed soon. It is easy to understand how hard it was for Mr. Johnson to spare the time just then, but he went to the funeral. I was there with him. The family of the dead man were greatly pleased because the President honored them, and the daughter thanked him touchingly.

As the trial proceeded, the conviction grew with me—I think it did with every one—that the weight of evidence and of constitutional principle lay with the defence. There were several clever lawyers on the prosecution, and Butler had his legal precedents skilfully marshalled, but the greater part of the proceedings showed personal feeling and prejudice rather than proof. Every appeal that could be made to the passions of the time was utilized. "Warren Hastings," "Charles I." "Irresponsible tyranny," were always on the lips of the prosecution.

In comparison, the calm, ordered, masterly reasoning of the defence must have inspired every one with a conviction of the truth of their cause. Their efforts were of varying ability and character, of course. The minds of these men were as diverse as their faces. Mr. Nelson was a short, stout man with a ruddy face. Mr. Evarts, who was then laying the foundation for his future unquestioned eminence, was an active, thin man. Mr. Groesbeck, who was ill during the trial, and was forced to have his clerk read his argument, had, with appropriateness, considering his name, a prominent, curved nose. Mr. Nelson's address was the most emotional of them all. His appeal was largely for sympathy, for admiration of the man Andrew Johnson; it was personal. Mr. Groesbeck was the surprise of the trial. He had been able to take very little part in the proceedings, but his argument was remarkably fine. Mr. Evarts's address was clearly reasoned. Mr. Curtis's argument, in my opinion, was the finest of them all.

But the legal struggle, after all, with that assemblage of violent passions was hardly the contest that counted. The debate was for the benefit of the

THE IMPEACHMENT

country at large; while the legal lights argued, the enemies of the President were working in other ways. The Senate was thoroughly canvassed, personal argument and influence were in constant use. Every personal motive, good or bad, was played upon. Long before the final ballot, it became known how most of the men would probably vote. Toward the end the doubtful ones had narrowed down to one man—Senator Ross, of Kansas. Kansas, which had been the fighting-ground of rebel guerilla and Northern abolitionist, was to have, in all probability, the determining vote in this contest.

Kansas was, from inception and history, abolitionist, radical. It would have been supposed that Senator Ross would vote with the Radicals. He had taken the place of James H. Lane, who had shot himself. Lane was a friend of the President, and, had he lived, in all probability would have supported him. But Ross had no such motive. It became known that he was doubtful; it was charged that he had been subject to personal influence—feminine influence.

Then the cohorts of the Senate and the House bore down upon the Senator from Kansas. Party discipline was brought to bear, and then ridicule. Either from uncertainty, or policy, or a desire to keep his associates in uncertainty, Ross refused to make an announcement of his policy. In all probability he was honestly trying to convince himself.

The last days before the test vote was to be taken were breathless ones. The country was paralyzed.

Business in the departments was almost at a standstill. Still, the President was the calmest man in the country, with interest to spare from his own affairs for those of other men. On the 14th he was visited by an enthusiast, Sergeant Bates, who had taken the Federal flag on a tour through the South to see whether he could prove that the South was loyal, and had walked to Washington from Vicksburg. The President gave him an interview. The man's enterprise evidently appealed to him. With a good deal of feeling and a clasp of his hand, he said, when Bates entered:

"I just want to welcome you to Washington."

Bates wanted to wave the flag from the top of the Capitol, but Congress refused. The President gave him permission to take the Stars and Stripes to the top of the unfinished Monument. At the last, Mr. Johnson put a purse into his hand, for all of Bates's expenses had been defrayed by the Southern cities through which he had passed.

On May 15th, a rainy, dismal day, the Lincoln Monument in front of the city hall was dedicated. Either the anxiety of Congress to have the impeachment over, or, more probably, a desire to show contempt for Andrew Johnson, who was to preside, caused both Houses to refuse to adjourn to honor the memory of the dead President. I accompanied Mr. Johnson and saw the exercises, which were finished without the recognition of our legislators.

On May 16th the vote was taken.

Every one who by any possible means could get

THE IMPEACHMENT

a ticket of admission to the Senate chamber produced it early that morning at the Capitol. The floor and galleries were crowded.

The journal was read; the House of Representatives was notified that the Senate, "sitting for the trial of the President upon the articles of impeachment," was ready to receive the other House in the Senate chamber. The question of voting first upon the eleventh article was decided.

While the clerk was reading the legal statement of those crimes of which, in the opinion of the House of Representatives, the President was guilty, some people fidgeted and some sat with their hands tensely clasped together. At the end, the Chief-Justice directed that the roll be called. The clerk called out:

"Mr. Anthony." Mr. Anthony rose.

"Mt. Anthony"—the Chief-Justice fastened his eyes upon the Senator—" how say you ? Is the respondent, Andrew Johnson, President of the United States, guilty or not guilty of a high misdemeanor as charged in this article?"

"Guilty," answered Mr. Anthony.

A sigh went round the assemblage. Yet Mr. Anthony's vote was not in doubt. A two-thirds vote of thirty-six to eighteen was necessary to convict. Thirty-four of the Senators were pledged to vote against the President. Mr. Fowler, of Tennessee, it was known, would probably vote for acquittal, although there was some doubt. Senator Ross was the sphinx; no one knew his position.

The same form was maintained with each Senator

in turn. When Fowler's name was reached, every one leaned forward to catch the word.

"Not guilty," said Senator Fowler.

The tension grew. There was a weary number of names before that of Ross was reached. When the clerk called it, and Ross stood forth, the crowd held its breath.

"Not guilty," called the Senator from Kansas.

It was like the babbling over of a caldron. The Radical Senators, who had been laboring with Ross only a short time before, turned to him in rage; all over the house people began to stir. The rest of the roll-call was listened to with lessened interest, although there was still the chance for a surprise. When it was over, and the result—thirty-five to nineteen—was announced, there was a wild outburst, chiefly groans of anger and disappointment, for the friends of the President were in the minority. [1]

---

[1] I find in my diary mention of a dream that I had on the night of the 26th of March. I thought that the vote on the impeachment had been taken and that the numbers were thirty-five for the prosecution to fifteen for the defence, with four absent. It is odd to notice that it was almost the actual vote. With the four who in my dream were absent added to the fifteen, it would have been the exact division of votes. I suppose it meant that I had been canvassing the probable disposition of the votes, and had repeated my guessing in my dream.

THE SENATE AS A COURT OF IMPEACHMENT FOR THE TRIAL
From a sketch made at the time for *Harper's Weekly* by Theodore R. Davis

VIII

AFTER THE IMPEACHMENT

I DID not wait to hear it, for, barely waiting for the verdict to be read—it was no surprise to me, as I had been keeping tally on a slip of paper—I ran down-stairs at the top of my speed. In the corridor of the Senate I came across a curious group. In it was Thad Stevens, who was a helpless cripple, with his two attendants carrying him high on their shoulders. All about the crowd, unable to get into the court-room, was calling out: "What was the verdict?" Thad Stevens's face was black with rage and disappointment. He brandished his arms in the air, and shouted in answer:

"The country is going to the devil!"

I ran all the way from the Capitol to the White House. I was young and strong in those days, and I made good time. When I burst into the library, where the President sat with Secretary Welles and two other men whom I cannot remember, they were quietly talking. Mr. Johnson was seated at a little table on which luncheon had been spread in the rounding southern end of the room. There were no signs of excitement.

"Mr. President," I shouted, too crazy with delight to restrain myself, "you are acquitted!"

All rose. I made my way to the President and got hold of his hand. The other men surrounded him, and began to shake his hand. The President responded to their congratulations calmly enough for a moment, and then I saw that tears were rolling down his face. I stared at him; and yet I felt I ought to turn my eyes away.

It was all over in a moment, and Mr. Johnson was ordering some whiskey from the cellar. When it came, he himself poured it into glasses for us, and we all stood up and drank a silent toast. There were some sandwiches on the table; we ate some, and then we felt better. In a few minutes came a message of congratulation from Secretary Seward to "my dear friend." By that time the room was full of people, and I slipped away.

Now I want to tell a very curious thing, which I did not understand at the time, and still can explain only by conjecture.

During the latter part of the trial, while Ben Butler was still apparently the President's bitterest enemy, and was making fierce attacks on him in the Senate chamber, many messages passed between the President and him of which nothing was known to any one but themselves and me. I was the messenger, and the letters were always sent at night. Mr. Johnson would call me to him and say:

"Crook, here is a letter for General Butler. I wish you would take it to him and wait for an answer." Although I can remember no positive direction from the President, my recollection is that these messages were not to be talked about. Sometimes the President would say:

"There is no answer."

General Butler lived on I Street, near Fifteenth. It was a short walk from the White House to his home. When I rang the bell, the butler answered it. He was a curious old chap, cross-eyed like his master. When there was an answer, I always gave it into the President's own hands. He always tore up the notes; I saw him do it.

It used to puzzle me a good deal. Why should Mr. Johnson and a man who was pleading so bitterly a case against him have this correspondence ? Why should President Johnson, who always kept every scrap of correspondence, even his bills, tear up these notes ?

Another thing: Not long after the trial was over, it began to be a matter of comment that Ben Butler had become a friend of the President. Mrs. Ann S. Stephens, a popular novelist of the day, who knew the President well, laughed about Mr. Johnson's "sudden and ardent friend General Butler." I don't pretend to explain these things, but questions will suggest themselves.

Was General Butler sincere when he denounced the President so fiercely, or did he think that the side of the Radicals was the popular one ? Since he changed front so completely, as there is evidence that he did, at what time did he change, and what was his motive? Is it possible that he felt that impeachment was going to fail and thought that it would be well to make friends with the winner?

After the excitement of the trial was over, we settled down into what seemed like quiet, although there were always things enough happening. Among others, it was discovered that William P. Wood, who was chief of the Secret Service in the Treasury, had offered $10,000 to N. M. Young, who had been Jefferson Davis's private secretary, for any letters he might furnish showing complicity between President Johnson and Davis.

Although the verdict had been with the President, the nation was by no means convinced. It must be remembered that almost two-thirds of the Senate had voted to impeach him. The Radical leaders were unremitting in their opposition. In a speech delivered on the 7th of July, 1868, Thad Stevens, after having stated that he had decided it Wo-s impossible to remove an executive by peaceful means, said that the only recourse from tyranny would be "Brutus's dagger."

In spite of his outward stoicism, the long strain of his position was beginning to tell on the President. He had had for three years a continued struggle, almost alone, to maintain his position. He was strong, but he felt his isolation. I believe the nearest approach to discouragement in Andrew Johnson's life came immediately after the verdict was rendered which acquitted him. Even he had not the slightest hope of re-election, and re-election alone could mean

AFTER THE IMPEACHMENT

full vindication. A telegram which he sent to a friend who had written to him with encouragement shows plainly his depression:

> The will of the people, if truly reflected, would not be doubtful. I have experienced ingratitude so often that any result will not surprise me. I thank you most sincerely for the part you have taken in my behalf; it is appreciated the higher because unsolicited. You have no doubt read in the morning paper Stevens's articles of impeachment, together with his speech thereon, in which he states: "The block must be brought out and the axe sharpened: the only recourse from intolerable tyranny is Brutus's dagger," which he hopes may not be used. How is it possible for me to maintain my position against a vindictive and powerful majority, if abandoned by those who profess to agree with me and be supporters of the administration? Such an abandonment at this moment, when the heaviest assaults are being made, would seem an admission that the administration was wrong in its opposition to the series of despotic measures which have been and are being proposed to be forced upon the country.

Mr. Stevens did not live long to fight for the cause which, in his own fierce way, he was convinced was the righteous one. He died in Washington two weeks after Congress adjourned. Mr. Johnson lived to fight longer.

As the summer burned itself out to autumn, the President remained in the country a longer time on our daily drives. Except when the children were with us, he was more sombre than ever. One afternoon when we were at the Soldiers' Home he strolled into a little vine-covered summer-house which stood at the summit of a gentle slope. I entered and stood with him. Below us lay, line upon line, almost as far in both directions as our eyes could reach, plain little white tombstones marking the graves of the Federal soldiers. We were both silent. At last the President said, under his breath:

"It's a city, Crook—a city of the dead."

That afternoon, when we were almost home, Mr. Johnson said to me, suddenly:

"Everybody misunderstands me, Crook. I am not trying to introduce anything new. I am only trying to carry out the measures toward the South that Mr. Lincoln would have done had he lived."

The last autumn that he was in the White House, Mr. Johnson secured my appointment as a third-class clerk, detailed to the Executive Office. I received the notification on the 21st of November, 1869. From this time promotion would depend wholly upon my own efficiency and faithfulness. My family thought that a great deal had been gained with that third-class clerkship. My case was a type of the President's attitude toward his subordinates: he always looked out for their interests. I went to him and thanked him for his efforts in my behalf. He said he was glad I had the place.

Somehow I had expected that there would be a change in Mr. Johnson's position after his victory over the Radicals. If I had thought of it, I might have realized that the two-thirds majority was still against him. The only difference was that when they passed measures over the President's veto it was without debate. There was no longer need for discussion. It does seem unfortunate that none of

AFTER THE IMPEACHMENT

them took the trouble to read his message protesting against the reconstruction measures. To me it seemed fine.

There was one difficulty, growing out of the division between the President and Congress, which I believe no other chief executive has ever had to contend against. It was virtually impossible for Mr. Johnson to have his appointments to office confirmed, unless the men happened to be in high favor with Congress. It was a peculiarly irritating situation. The President, however, robbed it of its most humiliating features by the frankness with which he accepted it. He announced that he could not recommend any man for position who could not place on file, together with the usual credentials, proofs that he could command enough votes to be confirmed by the Senate. One of the President's self-appointed advisers was in a great state of indignation over this.

"You ought not to make such a statement," he said. "It is an indignity for the President of the United States."

In answer Mr. Johnson smiled slightly. He was one of the men who see nothing humiliating in looking a situation in the face. He was practical about this, as about everything else. Since senatorial pledges must be had to secure the confirmation of appointments, he would give the men he wished to appoint an opportunity to secure the names. Therefore, part of the regular office routine was the consideration of the number of Senators whom a would - be collector or postmaster could marshal to his support.

Mr. Ross, of Kansas, the Senator whose vote had saved the President from impeachment, was at the White House a good deal during the last months of Mr. Johnson's administration. I knew Mr. Ross well. He was a well-looking man of medium height, slightly stooped. He always wore a frock-coat. He was concerned over some appointments in Kansas which he considered necessary for the welfare of his party. It was natural that he should expect help from the man he had saved, and for whom he was suffering. For no one to-day can understand the effect in Kansas of Senator Ross's action. It was hardly safe for any one to speak in favor of him or of the President. One lady, whom I still know, was in Lawrence, Kansas, at the time. Her husband happened to be in Washington on business during the whole period. This gentleman was in favor of Johnson, and therefore approved of Senator Ross's vote. His wife did not dare let any of her friends and neighbors know of the opinions of the family.

The President could do little to help Mr. Ross. The Senator had to rely, like every one else, upon what congressional support ho could muster, and he was naturally in bad odor in both Houses. As it happened, nothing could have saved Ross's political position in Kansas. I have been told that when he went home old neighbors would not speak to him. He found life in Kansas impossible. When he had entered the Senate he apparently had a great career before him. He was now made Governor of New Mexico. I believe he afterward published a news-

AFTER THE IMPEACHMENT

paper in Texas. But so far as I can understand, his life never fulfilled all it had seemed to promise. His vote for Andrew Johnson marked the end of his national career.

As Mr. Johnson's administration wore to its close, the daily mail brought to light many contrasting sides of human nature. A few men wrote to him, assuring him of their approval. Amos Kendall, the ex-Postmaster-General, who gave the land for Gallaudet College, the institution for the education of deaf-mutes in Washington, was one of these, as was "Sunset" Cox. A fine address of the latter, in which he said that Mr. Johnson's career was an example of "moral courage against party discipline," was forwarded to the President, and I pasted it in the scrapbook.

An echo of tragic things was the request made by Booth's noble brother, Edwin Booth, for the possession of the body of the murderer, lying all this time in an unmarked grave at the Arsenal. He asked with no spirit of bitterness, but with the deepest sadness, for permission to remove the body of the "poor misguided boy." The request was granted, and the family buried the body again.

A great many men made suggestions for the President's future guidance. Soon after General Grant was elected, one correspondent had the happy thought that if Mr. Johnson would only refuse to accept General Grant's resignation from the army, it would then be impossible for the coming President to be inaugurated, and Mr. Johnson would have things all his own way! Another guileless being sent a supposedly counterfeit bill by means of which he was convinced a gang of outlaws were endeavoring to seduce his honesty. He was willing to furnish further proof for the sum of $10,000. This communication was labelled a "confidence game," and the dollar was appropriated for charitable purposes. At intervals amateur detectives furnished information as to meetings of conspirators with schemes inimical to the President.

But by far the greater part of the letters were personal appeals for help. Helpless citizens of the Southern States, men and women, pleaded with their champion for aid. One woman, the last of a great line, begged the President to save her from being despoiled of the land on which her family had lived for generations. A widow, who said that he had before this furnished her transportation out of his own pocket, asked for further assistance. An old journeyman tailor who had once worked for Mr. Johnson sought for help, with an evident confidence that it would be granted: part of both feet had been carried off by a shell, and he wanted ten or fifteen dollars to take him back to his friends.

Simple pleas of this nature the President could and did answer; but to the great cry for help that went up from the whole South he was able to give only slight response. His hope had been, as he often told me, to "build up" the South. The accounts of riots, of violence, the insolence of negro agitators, like Hunnicutt, of Richmond, the wholesale pilfering of the land

AFTER THE IMPEACHMENT

by carpet-baggers, were agonizing to those of us who had lived among the Southern people and knew what they were suffering. The only power that was left to the President was the appointment and removal of the military governors. In some cases Mr. Johnson answered the cry for justice by removing the men who seemed to the people of several States responsible for the condition of affairs. It was, of course, the system of reconstruction that was to answer, not the governors; but the appointment of new men gave the sufferers a gleam of hope.

It is not wonderful that, with all these things to harass him, the President had to turn somewhere for recreation. It was to the children he went. It is a pleasing thought that Andrew Johnson celebrated his sixtieth birthday, in the closing months of the bitterest struggle ever waged from the White House, with a great holiday party for children.

It was on the 30th of December, and there were almost four hundred children present. Almost as many households had been in a state of excitement since the arrival of the truly magnificent cards of invitation. "The President of the United States" it was who desired their presence; no mere child was the host! Every child whose father had any share in the public life of the time and was not the President's bitter enemy, was there. All of Marini's dancing academy were invited, for there was to be wonderful fancy dancing in the great East Room. In the years that I had been at the White House—and almost every White House family has had its petted children—there has never been a children's party so wonderful.

Mr. Johnson received, with Mrs. Patterson and his grandchildren about him, and Mrs. Johnson came down-stairs for a glimpse of the pretty scene. This was, unless I am mistaken, the second appearance she made during her White House life.

The dancing was in the East Room. There were a great many square dances, and a few waltzes and polkas; but the fancy dances were the best. Marini's picked pupils showed their prettiest steps. There was the "Highland fling" of course, and the "sailors' hornpipe." There was a Spanish dance, danced by small Miss Gaburri in a Spanish dress flashing with sequins. Then there was a very sentimental affair— which all the children liked best because there was a "story" in it where one little girl postured with every evidence of languishing devotion, and another little girl circled coquettishly and tantalizingly around her. Pretty Belle Patterson danced prettily, but the stars were the Spanish dancer and little Miss Keen, who were particular friends of the Patterson and Stover children. At the end, the whole company, tots and big girls and boys, were lined up for the "Virginia reel." After that came "refreshments"— the real "party," most of the children thought.

After his frolic with the children, there was little that was not unpleasant before the President. Early in 1869 Hugh McCulloch resigned his position as Secretary of the Treasury. There was a large clique which was violently opposed to McCulloch. He was suspected of Southern sympathies—his home was in Maryland. There had been constant attacks upon him and endless appeals to the President to remove him. But Johnson was loyal to the man who, with Secretary Welles and Secretary Seward, had been faithful to him through the whole of his troubled administration. He sustained McCulloch, as he sustained his own reconstruction policy. I do not understand the secret of the opposition to McCulloch. He was an absolutely honest man; perhaps that is the reason he had so many enemies.

During the last two months Mr. Johnson sat at the White House waiting for the man whom he hated to take his place. Whatever personal resentment he may have had against his enemies was swallowed up at this time, I am convinced, by his sympathy for the struggling masses in the South. He has told me how he felt for them and talked of his own frustrated plans. His hatred of the Southern leaders—the "brigadiers"—was for the moment lost sight of, though it was by no means assuaged. He was calm, however, and, as usual, there was nothing in his manner to reveal his feeling. I could not trace a single line in his face to testify to his four years' fight. He went about his preparations for departure in his orderly, methodical fashion. All his bills were called for and settled long before he left the White House. The steamship companies evidently thought he would be in need of rest and recreation, for they vied with one another in offering him free transportation to any European port he might desire to visit.

He might well have wished to accept their offer, for he stood high in the opinion of European nations, and his trip would have been an ovation. But flight was not in his mind.

While the President was so unmoved, the rest of us were beginning to understand what it was that Congress had been doing. Whether public opinion had begun to change to any marked degree I cannot state, but the last public reception that Mr. Johnson gave was marked by a good deal of enthusiasm. Still, he was with the mass of people a very unpopular man.

During all the long contest, as far as I know, neither Thad Stevens nor Charles Sumner ever came to the White House. No one would have expected Stevens to do it; he was too bitter, too passionate. But with most people Sumner stood for calm and unprejudiced principle. One would have thought that he, at least, would have endeavored to have a consultation with the President, to have found out just where he stood, and why he believed as he did, before making him a target for daily denunciation. Of course, it is possible that there may have been interviews of which I knew nothing, but I do not think it likely.

Perhaps I was prejudiced against Sumner, knowing how he had opposed President Lincoln, and having seen how Mr. Lincoln felt toward him. In my opinion, Sumner made most of the trouble. Stevens did not have much weight. Every one knew that he was prejudiced and fierce, and they made allowances for that. But Sumner gave the impression of calm.

AFTER THE IMPEACHMENT

He was a gentleman, he had correct manners, he was well-groomed, he had learning. To a large element in the country he was a sort of god. Of course there were a few men who, like some one in the New York Herald, called him a monomaniac on the subject of the negro; and he did irritate the other members of his party by delaying legislation while he quibbled as to whether negroes should be so far distinguished from other men as to be called "negroes"—he himself referring to them as "unionists."

It was to the party of Sumner and Stevens that Andrew Johnson yielded on the 4th of March, 1869, when, a little before noon, he left the White House, and it was to a man by whom he considered that he had been betrayed. Mr. Johnson had refused to ride in the carriage with President Grant, as has always been the custom for the outgoing President. I have heard it said that General Grant refused to ride with him. I do not know whether that is true or not; it does not seem like President Grant, who was kindliness itself. But I do know that Mr. Johnson refused to ride with the new President. I heard him say that he would not do it.

So Mr. Johnson remained quietly in the White House while the inauguration ceremonies were in progress, gathering up his papers and making final preparations. He took away with him all the records of the office and the scrap-books which I had compiled. He said:

"I found nothing here when I came, and I am going to leave nothing here when I go."

When he left all the employees of the White House gathered on the portico to say good-bye to him. No one else was there. His friends and enemies alike had flocked to see the installation of the new President. The family had preceded him. With all the others, I shook his hand, and said:

"Good-bye, Mr. President."

"Good-bye, Crook," he said. "And God bless you!"

He went down to the carriage which was waiting to take him to the home of Mr. John F. Coyle, who was one of the two owners and editors of the National Intelligencer, one of the papers which had constantly supported the administration. Coyle was a brilliant man and a warm friend; he was perhaps the best friend whom the President had in Washington, and Mr. Johnson was very fond of him and of his family. Some one once laughingly asked him when he was going to "shake off this mortal Coyle?" He had no desire to shake him off. Mr. Johnson was a good friend.

Somehow, when Andrew Johnson left the White House I did not feel that that was the end of him. Yet, in a nation where the retiring executive is usually the only man in the country without a future, there apparently never was so dead a President. During the few days he spent with Mr. Coyle he was almost deserted. He had realized long before the end that his election to the Presidency, which was the only thing that would have meant vindication, was an

AFTER THE IMPEACHMENT

impossibility. But he was too vital a man to stop fighting.

Therefore, I followed with eagerness his career during the years that followed. Every one knows that when he returned to Tennessee he found himself hopelessly unpopular. Brownlow had seen to that. It did not seem to daunt Mr. Johnson in the least. He went to work to win back lost ground. Soon after his return to Greenville there was a United States Senator to be chosen. He sought the position. He was defeated in that. It was too soon. Again he went patiently to work. The same method of personal talk with the "plain people" which had brought him to the front before served him now. Little by little he regained his ascendancy over his State. In 1872 he was announced as candidate for Congressman at Large from his State. He conducted a campaign of public speaking, and again he was defeated, but by a smaller margin. When, in 1875, he came forward to claim the United States senatorship, he was victorious. That was not a bad record for a man who, at sixty, had retired from the White House unpopular and discredited.

It was not seven years after he had been on trial before the Senate that Andrew Johnson took his place as a member of the body that had judged him. Public opinion had travelled a farther journey than the years had done, for his entrance was the scene of a great demonstration. It was the opening day of the special session of 1875. The Senate chamber and the galleries were crowded. His desk was piled high with flowers. Possibly some of the children to whom he used to give nosegays from the White House conservatories were old enough to remember and to return the gifts in kind. Senator Wilson, of Massachusetts, then Vice-President, was, as President of the Senate, to administer the oath. As Charles Sumner's colleague, he had been Johnson's persistent enemy.

There were three new Senators to be sworn in, one of them Hannibal Hamlin. As Andrew Johnson's rival for the Vice-Presidency, he also had been an opponent. He took the oath before Johnson; but the name of the ex-President was called before Hamlin had gone to his seat.

The square, sturdy figure of Andrew Johnson advanced to the desk. The three men stood together before the multitude, who had only one thought: "How would he meet these men who had been his enemies? Would he take their hands?"

There was no pause, although to us who were looking on there seemed to be. Johnson put out his hand without hesitation or embarrassment, without apparent realization that there was anything unusual in the situation. He shook hands first with Hamlin, then, turning, with Wilson, who stood before them both. From floor and galleries went up a thunder of applause. Both Wilson and Hamlin were tall men, and Andrew Johnson was short, but to every one present there was no taller man in the Senate that day.

The oath taken, he went into the cloak-room to

AFTER THE IMPEACHMENT

avoid publicity. But there he was surrounded by Senators, every man eager to take his hand.

There was one man of those whom he considered his enemies whom Mr. Johnson had not forgiven. It was only a day or two after he took his seat in the Senate that he sent for me to come to his hotel, the old Willard, on Pennsylvania Avenue. I found him, on a nearer view, looking very little changed. He was older, of course; there was more gray in his hair; his whole face looked bleached. He seemed finer to me; not less strong, but more delicate. There were no more lines in his face: those that had been there were deeper graven; that was all.

I asked for all the family, and he told me what there was to tell. Mrs. Johnson, I knew, was still living, but poor Robert Johnson had died soon after his father returned to Tennessee. He spoke to me of them both. The grandchildren were growing up. He told me of his fight for election.

"And now," he said, "I want you to tell me where I can find notices about Grant in my scrap-books. You remember where you pasted them in. I don't." He got the scrap-books, and I put slips of paper in to mark the references he wanted. As I rose to go he said:

"Crook, I have come back to the Senate with two purposes. One is to do what I can to punish the Southern brigadiers. They led the South into secession, and they have never had their deserts. The other—" He paused, and his face darkened.

"What is the other, Mr. Johnson?" I asked.

"The other is to make a speech against Grant. And I am going to make it this session."

He made the speech in less than two weeks from that evening. It was a clever one, too, and bitter. Every point of General Grant's career which might be considered vulnerable was very skilfully attacked. The fact that he had taken gifts and that it was suspected he desired a third term were played upon. Yes; Mr. Johnson did what he had intended to do, and had been intending to do ever since he left the White House. He was the best hater I ever knew.

He went back home at the end of the session, and then to visit his daughter, Mrs. Stover, in eastern Tennessee. There, given up to the family associations he clung to, and with the grandchildren he loved, he was stricken suddenly with paralysis, and July 31, 1875, he died. It seemed as if, with his speech against President Grant, some spring of action which had kept him fighting broke. The rest was peace.

IX

WHITE HOUSE UNDER U. S. GRANT

A STATE of panic existed about the White House during the early months of President Grant's occupancy. Andrew Johnson and the new President had been such bitter enemies that we all fully expected to lose our positions. Our happiness was not increased by the brooms with which a thoughtful public flooded the Executive Mansion. These were addressed to the President and bore the legend:

Make a clean sweep!

It was probably a very humorous idea, but unappreciated by us. We eyed the wretched things vindictively.

We found very soon that, in fearing, we had understood neither General Grant nor the men with whom he had surrounded himself. As far as I know only two men were removed from the White House force. These were clerks who had been making themselves conspicuous for months with their personal abuse of General Grant. Mr. Robert Lincoln wrote to General Dent, the President's brother-in-law, in my behalf:

My dear General,—I am requested by Mr. William H. Crook to write a note to you on the subject of his being re-

tained as a clerk in the Executive Office, where he now is. This I do with great pleasure, and T can assure you that you will find him a man who will do well what is given him to do. I am well acquainted with him, as he was in the White House during the last two or three years of my residence in Washington, and I shall be very glad if he receives your favorable attention.
Very truly yours,
ROBERT T. LINCOLN.

I think, however, that my retention was due quite as much to the general fairness of the President and his secretaries as to outside efforts. As soon as the office was organized I was made General Dent's assistant in the reception - room. For months after the inauguration efforts were made to get the position away from me. The most persistent applicant was a West Point classmate of General Dent's. Not being able to get an interview with the President, the man one day wrote on his card:

> If I can prove that he is not a Republican, will General Dent give me his place?

I did not know at this time what it was about, but I did when I heard General Dent's verbal answer: "I do not know anything about Mr. Crook's politics; I know that he suits me. That is enough." And General Dent tore up the card and threw it into the waste-paper basket.

The organization of a reception-room was practically a new idea. General Dent, sitting at his desk, acted as a guard on General Grant's time. No one was allowed to enter the office unless the reception-

ULYSSES S. GRANT

From the original negative taken from life by Brady in 1864, now in the private collection of Frederick H. Meserve, New York City.

room was convinced that his mission was worthy of the President's attention. Formerly all this work had been done by the secretaries, who were consequently much interrupted in their work.

In many other ways the administration of the office was simplified and at the same time made more efficient. There were not as many records kept as under Mr. Johnson. While Mr. Robert Douglas, the son of Stephen Douglas, was nominally the secretary, three officers who had served on General Grant's staff—General Dent, General Babcock, and General Porter—were detailed from the army and did most of the work. This fact placed Mr. Douglas, as I have heard him say, "in a most unpleasant position." Robert Douglas since then has proved that this was due to no lack of ability on his part. After a successful career in North Carolina as United States Marshal, he has for years served the State as Supreme Court Judge. The assistant private secretary was Mr. Levi P. Luckey, a warm friend of Minister Washburne and of General Babcock. General Adam Badeau, who had acted as General Grant's secretary during war-time, had an unofficial connection with the White House. He was at work on General Grant's military history, and had been assigned a room and a clerk to assist him in arranging papers.

There was something about the President's office at this time which, to my way of thinking, suggested a military council. It was not that there were any of the trappings of war, for, of course, all three of the officer-secretaries wore civilian dress; nor was it in any special ceremoniousness of manner, for they were men of simplicity and geniality. It was rather in the fine, soldierly presence of the men, as well as in a sort of military exactness which pervaded the routine business. Both General Porter and General Babcock were handsome men, with commanding, erect carriage. General Babcock was not as tall as the other, but he looked every inch a soldier. General Badeau was not as impressive in appearance, although he was a clever man, and knew how to tell a good story. But I never had much confidence in the things he wrote. I believe there was some difficulty later on about his military history of Grant. I know personally of serious misstatements as to other subjects for which he was responsible. He always impressed me as being entirely self-seeking. It was plain to every one in the office that the President had the warmest friendship for both Porter and Babcock. Porter was one of the few men who could make the President laugh. General Grant was usually so quiet that, had it been another man, he would have seemed saturnine. With him it was merely—silence, and a silence that was more full of kindness and contentment than anything else. General Porter was a particularly good after-dinner companion; it is said that no one could tell a Dutch or Irish dialect story as well. That seems odd for a man who had the manners of a Chesterfield. Perhaps it was because of his stories that, when the President came down for a day from Long Branch—where he made his summer home—to attend a cabinet meet ing, General Porter was his frequent companion at the little bachelor dinner sent in from Wormley's. The two would sit over their cigars until late into the night, and General Grant would smoke many cigars and shake with laughter over Porter's stories.

I think that General Dent was inclined to be somewhat jealous of both Porter and Babcock. It was natural, perhaps, that he should feel so, for, having his desk in the reception-room, he was not as intimately associated with the President as were the two military secretaries. He was a trifle sensitive about not being as well informed as the other men. In consequence the newspaper reporters found him their natural prey. When they first came to him to find out about any matter, he would say:

"Oh yes, I know all about that affair, but I can't talk."

Then the shrewd scribes would pretend not to believe that he had any information, and, in order to prove that he did know, he would talk—and sometimes more than he should have done.

Whether the President was annoyed by this or not I do not know, but it was impossible for any one to see General Grant with either Porter or Babcock without knowing that he was genuinely fond of both men. He used to call Babcock "Bab," and was as affectionate with him as so quiet a man could be.

The general public, of course, saw very little of this capacity of the President for friendship and geniality. What most impressed them was his taciturnity. I have laughed many times over the astonishment of a Dutchman who came to the White House to ask some favor—probably a position—of the President. He was accompanied by a number of friends, who were exploding with consonants and ejaculating gutturals at a great rate, apparently to give him courage. They had much advice to give him. The comer of the reception-room in which they were gathered was buzzing with sound. At last the Dutchman was allowed to enter. His friends were just soberly preparing to wait for him when he came out. Again they crowded eagerly around him.

"Veil?—Veil?" they demanded, impatiently. The man didn't seem to know how to begin. He was looking dazed and puzzled. His friends pressed him: "Veil?—Veil?"

"Veil," he said, wonderingly, "I vendt in—^undt I game oudt!" They all departed, darkly muttering gutturals.

The President had probably told him that he would " look into his case." If he found it a worthy one, the Dutchman received what he wanted, I am sure. General Grant rarely promised anything to applicants. If he did promise, the man might be sure of his position. I don't believe that President Grant ever failed to fulfil a promise. Even William P. Wood—of whom I shall have something to say later on—recognized that. At the time Wood was making himself ready to undermine the President's position, if opportunity offered, he wrote:

General Grant is no coward. If he decides and promises you the appointment, it will be made.

WHITE HOUSE UNDER U.S. GRANT

In general, President Grant's manner to the persons who passed the scrutiny of the reception-room and were allowed to enter his office, was noncommittal. When, at the beginning of the second administration, I was put in charge of the reception-room, I had more opportunity to observe his methods. He sat erect at his desk, and allowed the man to set forth his case. He was a good listener, and his silence was receptive, inviting the applicant to state his position fully. The keen eyes of the President were on him while he spoke. After a time I grew to interpret General Grant's expression fairly well, and could guess with some accuracy how the applicant had impressed him. But the man himself was usually mystified until he heard from the matter later on.

As far as possible, the President guarded himself against personal appeals. He did this, as I believe, so that he could decide on the merits of the case, uninfluenced by feeling. The whole routine of the office was organized for this purpose. The secretaries disposed of a great deal of business without consulting him; only those cases which really needed his attention were submitted to him. The clerks in the office saw very little of him. When I was in charge, at the close of each day, I went to him with the papers that had been left with me and explained their contents. He listened in silence. Then he took the papers and considered them. When he had finished they were all returned to the officers of departments under which they came, some with indorsements in the President's handwriting. From one case which came under my observation I feel sure that when President Grant felt it necessary to refuse to hear personal appeals it was often in fear that, if he heard them, his judgment might be influenced by personal sympathy.

The case to which I have referred was that of an unfortunate woman from Tennessee whose husband had been imprisoned for violating the Internal Revenue laws. She had had one interview with the President, in which she had placed the matter before him, accompanied by a strong petition signed by her friends and neighbors. The President had referred her to the Department of Justice, but the Attorney-General had reported adversely upon it. Still she persisted in her attempt to free her husband. She begged for another interview with the President. He declined to hear her, saying:

"I cannot grant her petition."

Then she pleaded with me to take a message to him. I must admit she moved me, and I took the card on which she had written a few words. As he read them his eyes filled with tears. On the reverse side of the card he wrote:

I have tried to find something to justify your husband, but I cannot. It is painful to me to refuse you.

I could see how much it cost him to persevere in what he felt was the right course. His position was often a hard one. Many appeals were made to him which he could not grant—and the President was a tender-hearted man.

WHITE HOUSE UNDER U.S. GRANT

When a case did come to his personal attention, and when the plea was something that he could grant, he was soft-hearted enough. At one time a young woman called and said that she must see the President on important business. She seemed to be in great distress. I told General Grant about her, and he said that he would give her a few minutes. When she went into the room she was trembling. With a shaky voice she managed to tell him that the young man to whom she was engaged had lost everything, and that their marriage—which was to have been in a month or so—seemed impossible—"Unless —oh, won't you give him an appointment in one of the departments, and then we can be married, and we'll be—oh—so happy?"

The President smiled to himself. It was evidently a novelty to him to appear as a sort of Presidential Cupid. He was silent, while the girl blushed. Then he asked her if she had any papers recommending her lover. In answer, she said:

"I will recommend him," and handed the General the application which had been made out by the young man. With a little twitching of his lips the President gravely acknowledged her recommendation and wrote something on a card. He handed it to her, saying:

"Tell the young man to present this to the head of the department indicated, and I hope you will both be happy."

This young woman was quite the most interesting recruit, as far as my knowledge goes, to the great army of office-seekers which, gathering from all directions, bore down upon Washington. Their pressure upon the President was something beyond belief. I have been in the White House for forty years, I have seen the hordes that besieged both Lincoln and Johnson. I have never seen anything in their administrations that could compare with the situation under Grant. Nor have I seen anything like it since.

I don't know what the reason for this was, unless it was that the general disorganization caused by the war was just beginning to be felt. President Johnson had been so isolated both from the Republicans and the Democrats that I suppose there were not so many that felt authorized in claiming positions of him. But President Grant was the Republican idol, and all good Republicans who helped elect him moved down upon Washington, Because of the enmity between Grant and Johnson it was expected that General Grant would make a clean sweep. Their numbers were swelled by the disbanded Union soldiers.

There were various reasons why there were more of those who wanted positions than there had been under Johnson. Many of them had been retained in service during the reconstruction troubles that followed the war. When the last State had been readmitted, the army could be reduced to its normal size. Then, too, the soldiers who were mustered out at the end of the war had naturally tried first to take up again the work they had put down at the call to arms. Where they found that the places they had filled were taken by other persons, and where no other situations were to be had in the towns from which they had gone out, they naturally turned to the Government for which they had been fighting to give them a chance of earning their living. And they felt that their old commander-in-chief would understand their need.

It is not surprising, then, that the first chance for positions should have been given to the disbanded soldiers. The first necessity was theirs as well as the first right. In many cases they were disabled from more active work. Moreover, these were the men whom General Grant knew best. "A loyal Union soldier" was a name to conjure by. The President's letter-book is full of notes of this sort: ". . . The President hopes that in your selections you will give the preference to disabled soldiers wherever they are found competent." There was even a new bureau formed, called "General Service," to give employment to ex-soldiers. I remember how emphatic he was about a case which I happened to call to his attention. The man was a thoroughly worthy one, an old soldier. He had been employed at the Capitol for three or four years, but in one of the changes he had been dismissed. His recommendations were of the highest character. All this I learned after he had been waiting for several days for an opportunity to see the President, who was very much crowded just then with business. I told General Grant about it. He listened attentively, and then wrote on a card:

> The Postmaster-General will appoint this man if he has to discharge a Democrat to do it.

Just as, in filling minor positions, he thought first of the soldiers whose loyalty had been tested, so, in filling positions which called for military knowledge or for strictly executive qualities, he turned to those officers who had had an opportunity to demonstrate those qualities in their military careers. It must be remembered that most of General Grant's active life had been spent in the army or in training for it. His associates at West Point became the officers in the Mexican War, and the officers, on both sides, in the Civil War. No man ever had a keener appreciation of the ability of other men in his own profession than did Ulysses S. Grant. His Memoirs are full of his impressions of his brother officers, always keen, usually kindly, often enthusiastic, and, even when he is forced to be disapproving, entirely fair. No man was more generous. I know of a good example of this trait. On one occasion, when the President and his family were at Long Branch, he gave a dinner of about twelve covers to an Englishman who was touring the United States. In the course of the conversation the Englishman asked General Grant what he thought of Sheridan as a commanding officer. The President had been rolling bread-balls between his fingers, as I have often seen him doing when I had messages to take to him in the dining-room—a queer little habit it was. He dropped the ball he was making, and looked squarely at his guest.

"Sheridan as a commanding general," he said, slowly, as if he were weighing his words, "has no superior, dead or alive."

WHITE HOUSE UNDER U.S. GRANT

Considering this quality of the man, it is not surprising that Generals Porter, Babcock, and Dent should have been detailed to the executive office, or that Generals Schofield, Rawlins, and Belknap should have been at different times Secretary of War, or that territorial governors should have been from the army. At the beginning of his administration I believe that the President did not consider it possible that a great soldier could fail to be otherwise a great man. This fact explains much that follows.

The President has been much criticised for his cabinet appointments. It may be noticed, however, that no ex-army officer was appointed to a cabinet position other than that of war, nor were the appointments dictated by party considerations. In this the President showed the same desire to act on his own independent judgment that I have remarked upon in the smaller cases that came before him for settlement. Adam Badeau also comments upon it in his recollections of General Grant. The President's determination not to be ruled by party considerations or by outside advice led to an apparent haste and secrecy which really made a great deal of trouble. One of the men whom he wished to appoint to a cabinet position couldn't accept it because he had not been given time for arranging his private affairs. The appointee had seen the President the day before the position was offered to him. There had been a cordial conversation, but nothing had been told him of the honor the President had decided to bestow upon him.

Because of this same habit, Mr. Hamilton Fish, to whom the President offered the portfolio of state after the resignation of Mr. Washburne, at first refused to accept. It was necessary to send General Babcock on to New York to persuade him to reconsider his determination. In the first letter-book of General Grant's administration, which I have in my possession, is a copy of the note which the President sent to Mr. Fish. He says:

. . . Let me beg of you now, to avoid another break, to accept for the present; and should you not like the position, you can withdraw after the adjournment of Congress.

It was fortunate that he did prevail on Mr. Fish to accept, for the New-Yorker was perhaps the strongest of the cabinet officers. I used to see him often about the White House. He was a large, British-looking sort of man.

The many difficulties growing out of the frequent cabinet changes brought discredit upon the administration. It was said that President Grant had lowered the position of cabinet officer. It was said that, in the case of Mr. Washburne, who was first appointed Secretary of State, the President, knowing that what Mr. Washburne really wanted was the mission to France, had deliberately given his friend the most dignified position at his command with the understanding that it was to be held only long enough for Mr. Washburne to fill the department with his own political henchmen. Of course, this sort of a bargain is made every day, but it was rather curious for the

WHITE HOUSE UNDER U.S. GRANT

President to be, on one hand, accused of undue independence of his party, and, on the other, of undue subservience to mere political considerations.

The incident is rather a small thing, and would not be worth discussing were it not that it was one of the factors of public criticism which began almost with the administration. Of course, I know nothing directly about matters of policy. But there is a communication in the letter-book of which I spoke which was written by President Grant to Mr. Washburne about this affair. He alludes first to the fact that Mr. Washburne had given his ill-health as a reason for resigning the Secretaryship. The letter goes on to say:

> ... Our present relations have been such from the breaking out of the Rebellion to the present day, and your support individually and of the Army, and its cause, such that no other idea presented itself stronger to my mind in the first news of my election to the Presidency than that I should continue to have your advice and assistance. In parting with you, therefore, I do it with ... the hope that you may soon be relieved of the physical disabilities tinder which you have labored for the last few years.

Now it is possible that this letter was a political expedient. Badeau says that General Grant learned diplomacy while he was President. But my own impression of General Grant's truthfulness makes me believe that he would not have written as he did unless he meant what he said. Mr. Luckey said to me that he himself was very much surprised at Mr. Washburne's action. I believe Luckey, who was a sort of political confidant of Washburne's, would have known had his resignation been a prearranged matter.

Another cabinet position about which there was a great deal of discussion was that of Secretary of the Treasury. General Grant offered the position to A. T. Stewart, the famous New York merchant, feeling that a man who was able to manage a great business so successfully would be just the man with whom to intrust the disordered finances of the country. Now Mr. Stewart had made a ten-thousand-dollar contribution to a fund which was raised in New York about three years earlier to enable General Grant, a poor man, to run for office. It was therefore immediately stated by the President's political enemies that Stewart had bought the position. Later on, in the campaign for re-election, certain members of the opposition in their campaign speeches seem to have purposely misstated the facts. They stated that it was just two weeks after the President had accepted the gift that he offered the portfolio to Mr. Stewart. This is one of the first instances of the way General Grant's reputation suffered from unfounded rumors. There was much opposition to Mr. Stewart, led by Charles Sumner, and he was not confirmed. Mr. Boutwell was made Secretary of the Treasury.

If the President did make mistakes in making his cabinet appointments, they were the ones that were natural to his temperament and training. He did not consult others in making appointments, even the men concerned. He made his choice with military promptness, as he would have appointed a department commander during the war. As for his desire not to be bound by party dictation, it was certainly a wholesome thing in a day when party was supposed to rule everything. And whether it was true that there was corruption among them or not, at the time of their appointment they were all considered to be men of stainless honor. No man can be expected to know what may develop in another man's character. There were at least three men of great ability in General Grant's first cabinet. I have read comments on the lack of judgment shown in the selection of the whole number, but it strikes me that the cabinet compared pretty favorably with later ones that I have known.

It was just the same way about other actions of the President. Even in the first administration the criticism began. Of course, it must be taken for granted that I am somewhat prejudiced. I would like to know what man wouldn't be after a long and pleasant association with people like General Grant and his family. But there are many facts to bear out my opinion. I can't find, even after all this time, when I have had an opportunity to read what other men have thought about it, a single instance of public policy which really originated with the President which was not as honest and vigorous as the actions of his private life.

Take the difficulty with England which grew out of the Alabama claim, for instance. What government could better have steered its way through a delicate and even dangerous matter? Of course, General Grant had the advantage of the brilliant statesmanship of Mr. Hamilton Fish. But General Grant chose the Secretary of State, and they acted throughout in perfect accord. They carried the thing through successfully in spite of the constant opposition of Sumner, who was chairman of the foreign relations committee. Motley, the historian, had been appointed Minister to England at the wish of Sumner. He acted on the instructions of the Senator instead of following the policy of the President and the Secretary of State. The result was that the English people were much displeased by the arrogance he showed, and it seemed at one time as if there might be discord between the two countries. President Grant immediately removed Motley, which was the only possible thing to do under the circumstances. Secretary Fish and Sir Edward Thornton, the British Minister, were then able to work together to have a Joint High Commission meet at Washington to settle the dispute. The result was the Treaty of Washington, which submitted the matter to arbitration. At Geneva, with Charles Francis Adams as the arbitrator for the United States, after great danger of disagreement, the case was finally won for the United States. While the success of the negotiations was due in great part to Secretary Fish and to Mr. Adams, as well as to the fairness of the English Government, it must not be forgotten that President Grant's attitude throughout had been firm and dignified as well as entirely free from bitterness.

WHITE HOUSE UNDER U.S. GRANT

There was one matter of foreign policy for which I think President Grant has never received enough credit. That was, the part which Minister Washburne played during the siege of Paris in the Franco-Prussian War. We have all read how Mr. Washburne remained in Paris when the representatives of other nations—fearing, I suppose, to get their home governments into trouble—had fled. The story of his life during the siege is full of interest and excitement. It has, of course, been made public property; but any one who wants to know just how important a factor the American Minister was can get a pretty good idea from the Washburne correspondence in the Congressional Library at Washington. There he will find appeal after appeal—from the parents of young Americans travelling in Europe, to find out whether their children were caught behind the Prussian barriers, and begging the Minister to get them out; from some *comptesse* or *marquise,* pleading that *monsieur le ministre* will find Marie or François hidden away in the deserted *hôtel*, and save her or him from starvation; from charity workers, who had some case of destitution to report.

Mr. Washburne worked nobly to perform all these commissions, and to administer various relief funds that were placed at his disposal. He made for himself a place in the affections of the French people which no other American has ever held. Of course the United States, too, took a position before other nations which she had never held before. But it is President Grant to whom credit of the policy is due, for he cabled Minister Washburne to remain in Paris and do what he could to protect the Americans there, and Minister Washburne remained in Paris because President Grant cabled him to do so.

I have seen somewhere the statement that General Grant needed all the credit he could get from the Treaty of Washington, and from foreign relations generally, to counteract the effect of his misgovernment at home. I can't understand remarks like this. Of course, it was true that his administrations were marked by a long series of political scandals. Owing to this, he was practically powerless in the second administration. But in the first, when he really had an opportunity to show what he could do, he did a number of pretty fine things.

It was only the other day that one of our newspapers came out with a panegyric on the part President Grant had played in vetoing the bill authorizing an overgreat bond issue. The editor said that in doing so he had saved the country from dishonor, for the Government would not have been able to redeem the notes. The President had the same sense of scrupulous honesty in his standards for the public at large as he proved that he had in his own personal money affairs—proved when to do so made him— well, something like a martyr. He never failed to take a firm stand for sound money; he insisted on a gold standard for paying the national debt; he sacrificed his own family connections when, in the big gold speculation, he found that his brother-in-law was counting on his help to enable the Fisk-Gould-

Corbin combination to corner gold. The President ordered a portion of the Treasury gold sold, and Fisk, Gould, and Corbin went down.

With regard to the part President Grant played in the Civil Service Reform agitation, I feel that he did all that it was possible for a man to do during those years, for he asserted his principles vigorously; he carried them out as far as he could (I have already said that the spoils system did not obtain in the office of which I had practical experience), and when he finally gave Civil Service Reform up, in 1874, he did it because he saw that it was impossible to carry it out in the condition of public feeling at that time. Afterward, in answer to some criticisms. General Grant said that his critics did not understand the conditions against which he had to contend. It is certainly true that, with the exception of a few reformers like Carl Schurz, the mass of the Republican Party had no desire to have Civil Service Reform established. It is true that President Hayes and President Cleveland, later on, were able to accomplish more. But the public feeling was very different during their administrations. The display of public corruption had sickened the people and made them ready for reform.

If any one wants proof that President Grant was better than his party, all he has to do is to study the great Southern Pacific-Credit Mobilier steal which Congress allowed to go through. No one will ever know just how many Congressmen and Senators were bought by those expert "financiers." But that great numbers were presented with Southern Pacific stock, and that some of the greatest were implicated, there can be no doubt. That is a pretty good test of the state of politician morals. It shows, too, just how possible it would have been to get disinterested reform legislation through.

Whether the President was energetic in his Civil Service Reform policy or not, he was, as I have said before, most just and fair in his dealings with his own subordinates. The merit system certainly prevailed in the executive office, even if none of us had passed competitive examinations to get there. While President Grant was laconic to his clerks as to the rest of the world, I have reason to know that he was observant. Up to the end of the first administration I had never been particularly sure that he even knew that I was around. Yet when, in 1873, General Dent left the White House and returned to the army, the President arranged that I should have charge of the reception-room. I should never have known that I was promoted by General Grant's wish had General Dent not told me. Some time after I had taken my desk there I was home sick for two days. General Babcock told me that the President came in and looked around for me.

"Where is Crook?" he asked.

"He is home sick," General Babcock told him.

"I thought he must be away," said the President. "Nothing has gone right here these two days."

He paid us the greatest consideration that it is ever possible for a superior to show to his subordinates—a quick and business-like response when he was appealed to in our interest. An incident which happened after he left the White House will illustrate this point. In 1881, after Mr. Garfield was inaugurated, I asked General Grant for a letter recommending me to the new administration. General Grant was in New York at the time. I sent the letter Thursday. The answer came Saturday. At that time there could have been nothing kinder to me than such promptness.

Yet I do not think that President Grant was beloved by the people about him quite as President Lincoln was; in fact, no one ever had the marvellous power of attraction that Abraham Lincoln had. But we thoroughly respected General Grant. I can hardly express too strongly the confidence with which he inspired us all. We all felt instinctively that he was absolutely honest. With other men he was a square man.

X

FAMILY LIFE OF THE GRANTS

WITH the beginning of the second administration a decided change took place in the character of the executive office. The military element in it almost entirely disappeared. As I have said before, General Dent went back into the army; General Porter accepted a position as Vice-President of the Pullman Palace Car Company, and left us; while General Babcock still acted as Secretary, in 1871 he was made Superintendent of Buildings and Grounds, and discharged those functions in addition to his former duties. The public must have missed the military titles which had so abounded, for, as soon as I was placed in charge of the reception-room, they christened me "Colonel" Crook. And "Colonel" I have remained ever since.

It was natural that in the second administration I should have come more closely in touch both with General Grant and with his family. I wish to say here that, in the four years in which I saw him every day except Sunday, I do not remember one occasion when the President was out of temper or when he failed to listen sympathetically to all requests. Nor

FAMILY LIFE OF THE GRANTS

do I know of one case where he did not do all that he could for the applicant.

I think no man ever separated his business life from his social life more completely than did President Grant. He was an entirely different man when his friends were around him. That does not mean that he was talkative or that he laughed very often, but he was genial and full of content. And then again, no man ever kept his home more apart from both business and formal social things.

It surely must have done every one who was associated with the White House good to have it a real home. I know it did me. While the clerks saw little of General Grant, the relation between the President and his secretaries was so pleasant, and they in turn so passed on the kindly feeling, that somehow the whole force felt it. It warmed us all like a glowing fire. One illustration that I remember of the pleasant thoughtfulness shown by some member of the Grant family was the croquet-ground, which was given up to the use of the office force. It was laid out in the south grounds, near to the house. Any pleasant afternoon, after office hours, exciting tournaments were the order of the day. Major Sniffen, who was assistant private secretary in the second administration, and I were partners or competitors in many a close-drawn game.

The influence of Mrs. Grant, too, was felt more than had been that of the mistress of the White House before—as long, at least, as I had been in it. Mrs. Grant was a warm-hearted, kindly woman. She was familiar with the White House from cellar to garret, and she knew the servants personally. Her interest in her domestic household was not a perfunctory one; she had a motherly sort of feeling of responsibility in the welfare of her dependents. Any morning her stout, comfortable figure might have been seen making the rounds of kitchens and pantries, and stopping to hold little colloquies with maids or men. She was particularly anxious that the servants should be thrifty and saving. She urged them to begin to buy little homes, that they might be more independent and self-respecting. One of the footmen owes the fact that he owns the home he now lives in to her advice.

Moreover, Mrs. Grant had a great deal of influence with her husband. I saw an evidence of this one morning. A man called to ask the President for an appointment. He failed to see General Grant, but succeeded in getting an interview with Mrs. Grant, and in interesting her in his behalf. The result was that Mrs. Grant sent the man to her husband in my charge. With him was a card that read:

> Dear Ulys,—Do please make this appointment.
> JULIA.

The man received what he wanted, and I kept the card.

Yet no one obeyed the President's wife because she was haughty or particularly commanding; it was rather because she made persons want to please her.

The same thing was true, in different degrees, of

course, of the whole family. I have never seen a more devoted family or a happier one. There never seemed to be the slightest jar. To begin with, I don't believe any man and wife were ever more devoted than were the President and Mrs. Grant. I am sure he thought she was absolutely perfect. Why, when arrangements had been made to have a slight operation on Mrs. Grant's eyes to straighten them, at the last minute the General overturned everything. He said he wouldn't have anything done to the eyes. He liked her just as she was. The President couldn't get along without his wife. He wouldn't sit down to the table without her. In the morning he was always up first, and had time to read the morning papers— the *Republican* or the *Post*—before Mrs. Grant was dressed. But as soon as breakfast was announced, at half-past nine, he would knock at Mrs. Grant's door. Her voice would come from within:

"Is that you, Ulys?"

"Breakfast is ready."

"I will be there in a few minutes. General."

The General would walk to the window of the library and wait, fidgeting, until she joined him. Then she took his arm, and they went down to breakfast together. The children were usually there, but whether they were or not, one of these inseparables never thought of eating a meal without the other. The breakfast, as a rule, was plain—broiled Spanish mackerel, steak, breakfast-bacon and fried apples (a favorite dish), and rolls, flannel cakes or buckwheat cakes, with a cup of strong coffee. When the President had signified that he had finished by pushing back his chair, Mrs. Grant would look up and say:

"All right, Ulys, I will be through in a few minutes." Then, when she had had another half cup of coffee, she would take his arm again and they would go up-stairs to her room. There they always had a little talk to begin the day with, until he had to leave for his office in the cabinet-room.

At two, when lunch was announced, the President went to find Mrs. Grant in the library, where she sat crocheting or reading. Again they went arm in arm to and from the dining-room. After lunch General Grant drove in his buggy, walked, or rested a short time. At dinner the family was all together. They went down together at seven. It was a jolly meal, with a great deal of fun and laughter. Daily, when the President was through, he rolled up bread into little balls and aimed them at his two youngest children, Nellie and Jesse. When the missiles hit, he went over and kissed the victim on the cheek. He was a most loving father.

Mr. Frederick Dent Grant was away with the army most of the time, but his beautiful young wife was often at the White House. Mrs. Grant seemed devoted to her daughter-in-law, and had Mrs. Fred with her as much as she could. It was at the White House that the oldest child was born. Ulysses, the second son of General and Mrs. Grant, was a young man, and occupied with his own pursuits. But Jesse was a boy of about ten, and Nellie was one of the sweetest and most lovable young girls I have ever seen. There was something winsome about her. She wasn't exactly pretty, but I have never known any one who was more surrounded by the atmosphere of springtime and freshness.

Miss Nellie had been in Europe the year before her father's second inauguration. She was much petted there, and treated as if she were a little princess. Her father and mother were very lonely without her. They adored her. Mr. Luckey said that the reason they had sent her away was that they realized that she would be much sought, and they thought it best to keep her from youthful adorers as long as possible. That was an ironical sort of thing when one remembers that she met young Sartoris on the return voyage.

Old Mr. Dent, Mrs. Grant's father, lived at the White House until his death in 1873. He was a sociable and most lovable old gentleman. He loved to spend his time in the reception-room. There many of his old friends found him out when they came to Washington, and he could talk with them about Missouri and before-the-war politics. He admired his son-in-law, but did not at all approve of General Grant's politics. He called the President a turncoat. The reason of this was that, in 1856, he had cast his vote for Buchanan, feeling that the election of a Democrat would postpone secession, but that secession would certainly follow the success of the Republican Party. General Grant has explained this point in his Memoirs. But Mr. Dent could never understand the apparent change in party. He said that his children were all turn-coats, but that he himself never changed his colors. He never quite gave up the hope that the President would see the error of his ways and return to the Democratic Party. When President Grant signed the Fifteenth Amendment, his father-in-law said:

"Well, the Republicans are glad now to have the negro vote, but they will be damned sorry after a while." It was not long before the prophecy was fulfilled.

But the old gentleman did not live to know it. He died in December of 1873. There was no real illness; it was rather a general decay of the vital force. He sent for me the day before the end. He wanted me to make a memorandum of some "soldier scrip" he held for lands in the West. As I was about to leave the room, he said, rather cheerfully than otherwise:

"Do you know, Crook, I'm just like a candle? I'll snuff out." And the next day his life did flicker out.

The funeral service was held in the Blue Room. Reverend Doctor Tiffany, the pastor of the Metropolitan Methodist Church, preached the funeral sermon. It was one of the most beautiful addresses I ever heard.

Mr. Dent's death made a sad holiday-time. Mrs. Grant had been happy in the expectation of having her children all together again for Christmas, but grief for her father overshadowed everything. The New-Year reception was little more than a week off, and she was uncertain whether she ought to receive or not. All of the cabinet ladies but Mrs. Fish begged her to receive; they persuaded her that she had no right to indulge her own private grief—for the New-Year reception was an important function. Much against her will, Mrs. Grant finally consented to remain during the presentation of the Diplomatic Corps, the Supreme Court, and the members of the cabinet. She was bitterly criticised by the Washington Capitol for having done so. She said afterward that she wished she had followed her own desire in the matter. Mrs. Grant took no further part in social affairs for several months.

It was not long before the President and his wife were again called upon to face a loss, which was none the less a loss because it was not by death. That was the marriage of their daughter Nellie to Algernon Sartoris, an Englishman. There had been objections on the part of General and Mrs. Grant, but they had finally given their consent. The wedding took place on the 21st of May, 1874, at eleven in the morning. I believe there is an old superstition that May is an unlucky month for marriages. There certainly seemed to be no forebodings in this May wedding—or, if there were, they were not made known to us of the household. There must have been the keenest grief on the part of the father and mother. They were losing their daughter before she had fairly put away her dolls—she was not twenty at the time. I know it seemed a sad sort of thing to me, who was not of the family. Perhaps it was because it was such a pretty wedding that it seemed sad.

I have heard many accounts of Nellie Grant's wedding, and read others. They all comment on the magnificence, the richness, of it. But what most impressed me was the youth and beauty of it. Miss Nellie was the youngest, freshest little bride. Sartoris was a tall, large, well-set-up man, fresh-colored and well-featured—a gallant enough fellow for such a spectacle. There were many pretty girls among the bridesmaids. These were Miss Edith Fish, daughter of the Secretary of State; Miss Bessie Conkling, daughter of the Senator from New York; Miss Sallie Frelinghuysen, daughter of the Senator from New Jersey; Miss Lillie Porter, daughter of the Admiral of the Navy; Miss Jennie Sherman, daughter of the General-in-Chief of the Army; Miss Anna Barnes, daughter of the Surgeon-General of the Army, and a particular friend of Miss Nellie's; Miss Fannie Drexel, daughter of A. J. Drexel, of Philadelphia, and Miss Maggie Dent, cousin of the bride. They all wore white, as I remember, and the bride wore white satin with veil and orange blossoms, and I am sure that is as accurately as a man can be expected to remember ladies' dresses as long ago as that. I do remember thinking that they looked like angels as they came down the long corridor in advance of Miss Nellie and her father, they were all so fair and sweet.

One amusing thing happened just before the wedding which shows how democratic we all were then. A cabinet officer—naturally I won't say which one— came to me and asked me very seriously what I thought would be proper to wear at the wedding.

I thought at first that he was joking, and so said:

"I'm sure you know much better than I do, Mr. Secretary."

But he persisted.

"But what do you intend to wear, Crook?"

"I expect to wear my Prince Albert"—that was what we used to call frock-coats in those days.

"Then I will wear one, too," he said, and a rather ill-fitting Prince Albert he did wear.

The ceremony took place in the East Room. The place was a mass of flowers and plants. A platform was erected in front of the window which overlooks the Treasury Department. The spot where the vows were to be exchanged was marked by a great wedding bell of flowers. There Reverend Doctor Tiffany awaited the bride and groom; it was the same minister who had conducted the service for Mr. Dent.

What made the wedding prettier than any which has occurred since, prettier than any other White House wedding could possibly be—unless the Executive Mansion is again remodelled—is that the bridal party came down the old stairway which used to stand at the western end of the long corridor in full sight of the company in the East Room. We could see them approaching a long time before they crossed the threshold. To see them all walking down so solemnly, awe at the approaching ceremony in each girlish face, and Miss Nellie at the last, sweet and blooming, and confident of happiness—somehow I imagine the sight brought tears to more eyes than mine.

13

After his daughter had left the house on her wedding trip the General was missed. After considerable search he was found sobbing in his daughter's room, with his head buried in her pillow.

Years afterward, when Mrs. Sartoris had finally left the country for which she resigned her own that day, she was in Washington for a visit. I went to see her, hoping that she might remember me. As soon as she saw me she burst into tears. I stood there, wishing with all my heart that I had not come. She had not seen me since her wedding-day—I suppose I brought more of the past to her mind than she could bear. In a minute she was herself again, and spoke to me very sweetly. I have not seen Miss Nellie since. But some time after that, at one of the White House receptions, Mrs. Grant sought me out and introduced me to one of Mrs. Sartoris's children as one of their grandfather's secretaries—in which capacity I did once act for a short time.

It was very largely the simple kindliness which Mrs. Grant showed in this instance—and which they all had—that made the Grant family so popular socially. It was the gayest, brightest of administrations. They had known what it was to be hampered by narrow means; they had been through the terrors and anxieties of war; they were warm-hearted, hospitable people—both General and Mrs. Grant thoroughly enjoyed the opportunity of making their official home the centre of a large hospitality.

Two international events served to add to the social brilliancy of the Grant administrations. One was the coming of the English commissioners to deliberate concerning the Alabama difficulty and the Alaskan boundary. Their coming was the occasion of much entertaining. I imagine that while their husbands were busy with the political questions, the ladies were just as much absorbed in planning new costumes. But that wasn't anything to the excitement occasioned by the visit of the Prince of Wales some years before. Nothing else was thought of for weeks. There was a brilliant reception and ball given by Minister and Mrs. Thornton. The President was there, although he came late and refused to dance when he was urged to do it. Just why any one would have thought General Grant would dance is a mystery to me. The Prince made up for the President's absence from the ball-room floor, however, and danced tirelessly, like the boy His Royal Highness was.

The public receptions, even, had an informality that pleased people. The military aids that are so prominent a feature of the state receptions now were absent then; there were not as many uniforms to be seen among the guests. The United States Marshal who introduced the people to the President and his wife was a brother-in-law of the President; Miss Nellie, during the few times that she was present, wore always a simple white gown; Col. Fred Grant's handsome young wife was often there—somehow the reception had the air of a family party.

While there were not as many state dinners as during the preceding administration, there were more unofficial affairs. General Grant particularly loved to have a few friends to dinner. He gave everything a more personal character than it had had before—during my experience, at least. He chose the wines himself, and gave directions that they should be of the proper temperature. General Grant was an open-handed, lavish host. I remember one wine bill which impressed me very much at the time—$1800 for champagne alone. One homely instance will show the President's position in domestic matters. Mr. Borie, the Secretary of the Navy, had sent General Grant some particularly fine wine, which was stored in the attic. It was to be brought out for one of the big dinners, and the President went himself, with Henry and Edgar, two of the servants, to have it drawn off into eight large decanters. On the way down Henry stumbled and fell, breaking the four decanters he was carrying. The President turned and looked at him, but didn't express his feelings further. When they got down - stairs General Grant said to Beckley, the steward:

"Get four other decanters and go to the garret and fill them, but don't let Henry go there again!"

Poor Henry confided to me afterward that when the General" looked at him" on the stairs he " thought he would go through the floor." It was such an unusual thing for the President to find fault with a servant that it made a great impression on him.

XI

POLITICAL DISSENSION

WITH the politicians President Grant was, unfortunately, not as popular as he was with his friends. He had not been President two years before the various centres of discontent began to organize in a concerted movement against him. When, in the second administration, there began to be rumors that he was hoping for a third term, his enemies were hysterical.

There were many factors in the opposition to General Grant, and many causes for the antagonism of each factor. First there was Charles Sumner, who had been an enemy almost from the beginning of the first administration. He had, of course, causes of complaint—honest differences of opinion with General Grant. But, more than that, he was an idealist, who had grown into a chronic state of disgust with everything. It will be remembered that Sumner had criticised Lincoln sincerely, that he had not been loyal to him. Sumner also considered Johnson personally beneath his notice, and fought the man's measures with vehemence. It seemed impossible for Charles Sumner to concur with the Government. Had he been an Englishman he would have been in variably a leader of the opposition. Moreover, in at least one matter—the Alabama affair—it is evident that President Grant and Secretary Fish were right and Sumner was wrong. Greeley was another man who was born to protest. Carl Schurz was an idealist who was pledged to oppose autocracy and corruption wherever he found them. Both of these evils he considered to be represented, at this time, by President Grant.

Among the President's enemies there were several who were possibly not as disinterested in their opposition as were Simmer and Schurz. Mr. Wilson, Mr. Simmer's colleague from Massachusetts, was generally considered to desire the Presidential nomination. Senator Trumbull was another Presidential possibility. He had been one of those who voted against the impeachment of Andrew Johnson, and had naturally inherited opposition to General Grant. Just before the Cincinnati convention in 1876 Senator Trumbull's friends talked of him for General Grant's successor. It was generally under-stood that the convention would nominate either Trumbull or Charles Francis Adams. I do not know whether Senator Trumbull really hoped for the honor, but he conducted a modest sort of a campaign. He wrote to his supporters in terms which suggested disapproval of the present administration, and signified that there might be found an honest man who would unite the disaffected Republican element—the Liberal Republicans—with the Democrats. Horace Greeley also wanted the position. To the amazement of every-

POLITICAL DISSENSION

body but his lieutenants, he received the nomination of the Liberal Republicans. According to agreement, he was accepted as candidate by the Democrats.

Just how far these opponents of General Grant's, interested or disinterested, were responsible for the great epidemic of distrust that swept over the land in the second administration I have no way of knowing. I am sure there is no doubt that they were to some extent responsible. The first three years of the first administration had been prosperous. Certain political scandals were developed, but there was nothing for which any thinking man could consider the President responsible. Then the leaders of the Liberal Republican movement began to circulate stories of corruption. As far back as 1870 Senator Sumner had charged General Babcock with corruption in such a way as to reflect on the President. At this time there had been nothing against Babcock's reputation. Sumner was merely angry with him because Babcock's report on the San Domingo annexation project had been favorable to the President's desire for annexation, with regard to which Senator Sumner was opposed to President Grant. The Liberal Republicans enlarged upon the various political scandals until they made their constituents believe that the President was responsible for measures which were entirely due to dishonest men in Congress. They misrepresented, as I have already said, the matter of A. T. Stewart's connection with the fund presented to General Grant. Whether the President's enemies believed the charges that they made or not, their reiteration of these stories of corruption created a general condition of distrust which had much to do with the great panic of 1873, in which so many fortunes went down.

In spite of their activity, the opposition could not carry the election. The defeat of the Greeley party in 1872 proved singularly disastrous. It was doubly fatal to Greeley himself. It was generally believed that he was killed by ridicule. It is certain that Nast's cartoons were particularly savage. Greeley's personal peculiarities were irresistible to a fun-maker. The caricatures of his figure and his long whiskers, as Nast drew them, were equal to arguments against him. I remember one of Nast's cartoons that went all over the country. In it Grant's head—more impressive than in life—was protruding from between the curtains of an old-fashioned four-poster bed. There was an expression of fierce indignation on his face while he surveyed Greeley, just in the act of stealing the President's boots. Grant was supposed to be calling out, peremptorily:

"Drop them!"

The election forced poor Greeley to "drop them." The circumstances of his life aggravated his natural disappointment. Before the election he had spent sleepless nights beside the bedside of his dying wife, whose last days were embittered by the abuse and ridicule that were being heaped upon her husband. After his defeat he returned to his lonely home and to his crippled newspaper. He tried to take up his life again, but he was worn out by grief and over-

POLITICAL DISSENSION

work, and wounded by the things that had been said and written about him. Less than a month after the election he died, a broken-hearted man.

Charles Sumner, too, was a wreck of the election of 1872. When he went home to Massachusetts, his constituents and neighbors were so indignant with him and his desertion of the Republican Party and alliance with the Democrats that he was publicly reprimanded. This disgrace for the proud man who had been the idol of his State, and at one time of his party, together with his own domestic unhappiness brought him into a state of intense despondency, which was one of the main causes of his death.

Some men say that the election of 1872, in which General Grant won rather by the weakness of his adversary than by his own strength, proved the cause of the death, not of his body, but of that greater thing: his claim to the respect of his countrymen; for it was in the years of his continued lease of power that the great scandals culminated which made men say that President Grant, even if he were not himself dishonest, was ruled by men who were. It was in the second administration that Belknap was Secretary of War, and it was in 1875 that the Whiskey Ring conspiracy was first suspected. These two things alone, they say, have destroyed General Grant's reputation as an executive.

I do not agree with these critics of President Grant. I believe that the mistakes he made were on the side of greatness. Mere keenness of insight is not as great a thing as the capacity for belief in a man when appearances and the majority are against him. General Grant was loyal to both Belknap and Babcock when to be loyal meant his own political ruin. He has been generally blamed for his support of them. I admire him for it. I believe, moreover, that there were more reasons for his action than have yet been made public.

With regard to the Whiskey Ring scandal, which involved General Babcock as well as a group of men not officially connected with the administration, while this is not the place to discuss it, there are certain things that have weight with me.

President Grant believed so strongly in General Babcock's innocence that I couldn't help thinking that there must be some good reason for it. I have heard it said that General Grant was blind where his friends were concerned. But he wasn't blind toward the disloyalty of other men who proved false to him during the eight years of his Presidency. There are several instances of his severity where he found he had been betrayed. The case of Postmaster Jewell, in the second administration, was one of these. When Mr. Jewell's resignation was asked for there was agitation in the newspapers and throughout the party generally. The query, "Why did the President demand Postmaster-General Jewell's resignation?" for a time took the place of "What has become of Charley Ross?" which was the mystery of the day. Mr. Jewell himself did not assign any reason to the newspaper reporters who went to him. An experience of mine may throw some light on the matter.

POLITICAL DISSENSION

The President had a fashion of writing recommendations with regard to appointments on cards, and sending them off to the various heads of departments. It happened that one man whose appointment had been recommended in this way to Postmaster-General Jewell did not receive the appointment, as he had expected. He came to me with his complaint— for I had been interested in his case, and had sent him to the President. It seems that Mr. Jewell had, in his presence, torn the card to pieces, saying:

"Grant hasn't any influence in this department."

I had heard of other instances of the same thing. It didn't seem to me that that was quite the fashion in which recommendations of the President of the United States should be treated. I advised the man to go in and tell the President his story. The result was that General Grant investigated the matter. The next day Postmaster-General Jewell was asked to resign.

Therefore, it meant a good deal to me when the President continued to believe in General Babcock after everything had been brought against him that could be brought.

Then, too, for my part. General Babcock always seemed to me to be an honest man—an honorable and a high-minded one. Again, I must admit that it is possible that I may have been prejudiced in his favor. General Babcock was very kind to me on more than one occasion.

One of these times was when a celebrated lawyer came into the office and told us of a marvellous mine in which he was interested. It was the chance of our lives to make a fortune, he said. I had no money, but I was so anxious to have a share in this "sure thing" that I asked Mr. Babcock if he would advance me the money. He loaned me a thousand dollars with only my note as security. I paid it back by degrees. As it turned out, not only that money was lost, but the stockholders lost by later assessments. I think that the man who got us into it believed fully in his mine, but it was rather hard on all of us. However, the point of the story is that General Babcock was a friend in this case.

The General was not a man who seemed to care particularly for luxury—there was no motive of that sort to fall from honor. He showed no signs of sudden wealth in his manner of living. He certainly never, as far as I know, sported the diamond that MacDonald was supposed to have given him. If the general opinion of men who were merely onlookers but closely associated with the principals is of any value, it was generally believed about the White House and other Government departments that General Babcock was innocent. Moreover, it was generally understood that Secretary Bristow, to further his own Presidential aspirations, aimed to discredit Grant by destroying Babcock. Every one thought that he wanted the Presidency, and was playing the part of reformer to catch the popular favor. This was an easy role, for the people at large were sickened by stories of corruption.

Personally—I might as well state it at the outset—I disliked Mr. Bristow. He was a big, beefy, over-

POLITICAL DISSENSION

grown man who seemed to me to be trying to bully every one. But his man Friday, Bluford Wilson, the Solicitor of the Treasury, was worse than he. We all thought that Wilson did the dirty work for Bristow. He looked the part. He was small and dark and secretive—a real human weasel, was Wilson. This may be all prejudice on my part, but see the part the man played in the whiskey prosecutions! And by means of the whiskey agitation, Bristow and Wilson exalted the dishonesty of a few corrupt men into a national conspiracy while they themselves posed as reformers. They were very nearly successful; but they overreached themselves. Senator Sherman said, before Hayes was seriously considered, that Bristow would have been the logical candidate in 1876 had any one believed that he was honest. And it was during the latter part of the whiskey prosecution that Bristow revealed himself.

At the beginning of the trial the President heartily co-operated with Secretary Bristow. In fact, as I have said, Bristow was promoted from a subordinate position in the Treasury with the distinct idea that he was zealous and would bring about much-needed reforms. It was not only the President who felt this, but his private secretaries, the very men who were afterward accused of being in collusion with the Whiskey Ring, and, like Avery, of furnishing information, I have seen a letter from Luckey written to Minister Washburne, in which he says:

> Mr. Bristow is starting in on his good work in the department, and will purify it.

The first cause of friction between the President and his reforming Secretary occurred in consequence of a remark made by ex-Senator J. B. Henderson, who had been appointed special counsel for the Government in the trial of Avery. Henderson hinted at the President's complicity—with Babcock—in the whiskey frauds. The President naturally demanded that Mr. Henderson should be removed, and was supported by the opinion of the whole cabinet. While Bristow, as a member of the cabinet, was forced to concur in this, Bluford Wilson, his mouthpiece, protested against Henderson's removal, taking the remarkable position that the success of the Government's case depended upon his serving. Henderson, of course, was removed.

The next matter in which the Secretary and Bluford Wilson showed their colors was in relation to the Barnard letter. Barnard had written to Bristow, and Bristow had submitted the letter to Grant, in reference to the whiskey trials and to the charges against Babcock. His letter was of no special significance, but General Grant wrote an indorsement on the back:

> Let no guilty, man escape if it can be avoided. Be especially vigilant—or instruct those employed in the prosecution of fraud to be—against all who insinuate that they have high influence to protect them. No personal considerations should stand in the way of performing a public trust.
>
> U. S. GRANT.

This perfectly clear statement of the position of an honest man, Bristow and Wilson—wherever they could without detection—reported, was obtained from the President with great difficulty and with every sign of anger. Afterward, under the Congressional examination, Bluford Wilson could not remember having made such a statement.

A far more serious disagreement arose between Secretary Bristow and the President over the manner of conducting the St. Louis trials; for Bristow and District-Attorney Dyer desired to allow the mass of the thieves to go free, provided they would turn state's evidence and testify against some one else. Joyce states that he was promised immunity if he would testify against Babcock. This offer was said to have been made in an interview with Bristow, in which the Secretary told Joyce that he really had a great regard for him and didn't want to see him get into trouble. Joyce's word alone would not be conclusive, but it was backed up by the testimony of many of the witnesses at the trial. Joyce had enough manhood not to be willing to save himself by turning traitor. He refused Bristow's offer and went to prison.

The practice of allowing the humbler criminals to go free providing they would testify against the greater became so generally used that the President's attention was attracted, and he became very indignant.

"I cannot see why nine thieves should go unpunished in order to catch the tenth," he said.

That Bluford Wilson did all he could to make it the purpose of the prosecution not, primarily, to secure justice, but to inculpate General Babcock and Luckey, and, by implication, the President, was proved by a letter which was written by the Solicitor of the Treasury to General Henderson while he was still the prosecuting attorney. In it Wilson suggested that it was necessary to look for the real offenders in the "W. H."— by which he of course meant the White House. In the Congressional investigation, when the letter was made public, Wilson attempted to prove that the letter had been tampered with, and "High up" changed to "W. H." But I think nobody believed him.

It cannot be imagined that the President could have honorably taken any other course—had General Babcock been his enemy instead of his friend—than to protest against such methods as these. And protest he did, by causing the Attorney-General to write a letter to the counsel expressing disapproval of their course. No one of General Grant's straightforward temperament could have done otherwise. The prosecution's method of inviting perjury threw discredit upon the earlier trial, and made it impossible to accept without question most of the testimony that led up to the indictment of Babcock.

Whether, therefore. Secretary Bristow believed in General Babcock's guilt or not, his methods were equally questionable. In interviews with newspaper correspondents and with the general public, while he protested his belief in the innocence of the President so loudly as to call universal attention to the charges, he managed to convey the impression that he was shielding a superior to whom he owed official allegiance. He harped upon the inside knowledge

POLITICAL DISSENSION

which, he claimed, Babcock possessed, of executive actions, in order to convey the impression that such knowledge could be explained only by there being guilty collusion between General Grant and his private secretary.

In the Congressional investigation that followed the trial Bluford Wilson was discredited, in the mind of every man in the city of Washington. He attempted to deny having made the statement with regard to the reluctance and anger with which General Grant had written his famous "Let no guilty man escape." But there were too many witnesses to his having made the charge to allow his denial to stand. Another transaction was laid bare. When Wilson left the Treasury—as he was obliged to do soon after the St. Louis trial—he attempted to keep, among the papers that he packed to take away, the Barnard letter with its indorsement. One of the men in the office informed Assistant Secretary C. C. Sniffen (now Paymaster-General, U. S. A.), who immediately sent an order that no official papers should be taken away. I presume the letter would have been conveniently "lost" had this action not been taken, and, with it, a valuable proof of the President's integrity. It was shown that Bluford Wilson had ordered three boxes of papers sent to his home, among them many documents which belonged to the Treasury Department. He stated, in defence, that this was owing to the mistake of a subordinate.

Another misstatement for which Wilson had been responsible was disproved. He had attempted to provide a motive for Babcock's supposed attempt to make money out of the Whiskey Ring by circulating the report that Babcock, as well as Porter, had lost in the "Black Friday" gold speculation. Porter proved that he had no connection with it, and Mr. Wilson had to confess himself ignorant of the fact that General Babcock had been in San Domingo on a mission for the President during the whole period. It was also developed that Wilson—acting for Bristow —had attempted to fasten complicity in the whiskey conspiracy on both General Logan and Farwell. General Logan, it must be remembered, was a widely popular war hero, and had been spoken of in some quarters for the Presidency.

As for Secretary Bristow's own Presidential aspirations, there can be no doubt that they existed, and that they furnished the motive for his attitude toward Babcock and President Grant. In addition to all this indirect proof, it was developed, also in the Congressional investigation, if I am not mistaken, that Bluford Wilson had told one of the revenue officers— subordinate to the Treasury Department— that they must "stop that damned Blaine business," which meant, of course, the Blaine boom. The man testified that this was told in such a manner that he considered it a threat. Wilson also said that Bristow was the man for President and they proposed to make him so.

At one time it had appeared that Bristow would be successful. He was praised as all that was the opposite of the reported corruption. But his con-

POLITICAL DISSENSION

duct of the whiskey trials, and the consequent disclosures of the investigation, killed his political hopes. He made as poor a figure in them as Wilson had done. He had pleaded that, as a cabinet officer, he was pledged to secrecy, and so could not speak of what had passed between the President and himself. But the President, with characteristic directness, published an open letter to him removing all restrictions. So he couldn't shelter himself behind that excuse, and pretend that "if he could tell all" it would be very dark for President Grant—very dark indeed!

Whatever his convictions—and it is quite probable that Bristow did believe in the guilt of Babcock— it was true beyond a doubt that Secretary Bristow had used the whiskey scandals to promote his own ambitions and to destroy the man who had confided to him one of the highest positions in a President's command. He was proved also to have used—or to have connived at—dishonorable methods. He was lowered in the general estimation.

I know I had been hoping pretty vigorously, long before this stage in the proceedings, that the President would understand both Bluford Wilson and Secretary Bristow, and protect himself. I believe I stated that I disliked Mr. Bristow. I felt that he was traitorous to the President. I wanted to tell the President so, but, of course, I couldn't say anything. If a subordinate like myself had dared to speak to General Grant of such a matter, it would have seemed like presumption, and I would probably have lost my place. Yet when Mr. Bristow would come to the White House for a conference and bring Wilson, and Wilson would watch the President, trying hard to hear a word that he could distort into something hurtful to that frank and generous man—well, it was hard to keep still.

So one day when General Grant called me to him and told me to go to Bristow and ask him to come over, I stood there with the words on the tip of my tongue, and trying hard not to let them get out. Then the President raised his eyes. He looked angry clear through.

"And tell Mr. Bristow," he added, and his eyes gleamed as he spoke, "not to bring that"—he hesitated a moment—"that Bluford Wilson with him again."

I went off, feeling that he was beginning to understand. I imagine I walked rather jauntily over to the Secretary's office. When I stood before Mr. Bristow I repeated the message. I said it word for word, and I reproduced the President's tone, too, pretty accurately. Nobody on the stage could have done it any better. Bristow evidently felt just what I was so pleased to convey. He turned fiercely red, and hadn't a word to say. But if my position had been in the Treasury Department my head would have been off before night.

A short time after this Secretary Bristow resigned his position and went to New York to live.

After the St. Louis trial General Babcock came back to the White House and held his position as private secretary there just long enough to demonstrate to the world that the President believed in his innocence. It was, of course, impossible for him to hold it, since many persons believed him guilty. He filled for a short time his old position of Superintendent of Buildings and Grounds, while Mr. Luckey was appointed Secretary of the Territory of Utah. I have several letters from Mr. Luckey, which he wrote me while he filled that position, describing the conditions in the Mormon State. The secretaryship was filled by the President's son. Ulysses was a good secretary. He was like his father in temperament, and much beloved. The reason of this fact is not far to seek when one recalls incidents of his thoughtfulness. While the family was away in Pennsylvania, during the summer of 1876, when I was acting secretary, I received, of course, a good many letters from both General Grant and Ulysses. In one of the latter's notes he asked me to have flowers sent regularly to them from the White House conservatories. And in the postscript he says:

Order some for yourself whenever you want them.

Immediately after the verdict of acquittal of General Babcock at St. Louis, a second attack was made upon him. This time his honesty as Superintendent of Buildings and Grounds was questioned. I think it will be felt that I am not overstating the case when I say that disclosures made in connection with this affair show that a conspiracy against him undoubtedly existed. And the object of that conspiracy of General Babcock's enemies was to complete the ruin that the whiskey trials had begun.

The attack began by a charge that General Babcock had submitted false measurements. In producing answer a book of evidence was submitted by a man named Evans. This evidence was assailed by the prosecution as not being the original book, but a falsification. It was, in common with other evidence in the case, in the possession of Harrington, the Assistant District Attorney. Suddenly everybody was startled by the news that the office of Harrington had been opened, the safe rifled, and the evidence against Babcock removed. The statement was immediately circulated that Babcock had caused it to be done to destroy incriminating evidence. The public was, very naturally, ready to believe it because of the dubious light in which General Babcock still stood. The robbery occurred on the 10th of March, about two weeks after the verdict at St. Louis.

While these rumors were in the air, an article appeared in the New York Sun charging that a man named Whitley, the Chief of the New York Secret Service— who had very recently been displaced as Chief of the Secret Service in Washington—was connected with the safe burglary. Whitley came on to Washington. He asked for immunity if he would tell all he knew. Before the District Attorney he stated that he had performed the robbery at the instigation of General Babcock. On the 16th of April General Babcock was indicted, with Harrington, for complicity in the

POLITICAL DISSENSION

safe burglary. The trial went over until the following September,

At the trial in September the accusation dwindled down in the most amazing manner. Whitley began bravely enough by stating that he had undertaken the matter at the request of Babcock. He had employed several men, some of them detectives, and some of them expert burglars whom the Chief of the New York Secret Service knew, apparently, how to make useful. The object of the burglary, Whitley stated, was to steal the Evans evidence, take it to the prosecution with the statement that it was the real, not the spurious evidence, and submit it. This was to "turn the laugh" on the prosecution when they had accepted what they before had declared a falsification. It is amazing that any sane man could have thought a tale like this would be believed.

Under cross - examination Whitley broke down completely. He was forced to admit that he had been promised immunity in return for testimony against Babcock. He could prove collusion with no one but Harrington. The only proof of collusion with General Babcock was that, when on one occasion he had gone to Babcock to get his assistance in collecting back pay, Babcock had sent him to Harrington; and Harrington was the man who had proposed the plan to him. Whitley had "inferred" that the scheme was Babcock's. In short, Whitley revealed himself to be a tool for sale to the highest bidder, and for use in any rascality. The trial closed with a vindication of General Babcock. But it left every one confused as to the motive that could have induced Whitley and Harrington—if it were true that Harrington was really involved in the matter at all—to undertake such a project. Nor could the public understand why a man who had had experience in criminal cases could have made a charge against General Babcock when he had nothing with which to support it. Some time after this all happened I got possession of a letter from William P. Wood, a former chief of the Secret Service in the Treasury Department. He was the man who, in the administration of Andrew Johnson, was discovered to have offered $10,000 for letters proving collusion between Jefferson Davis and Johnson. Wood had been dismissed from the service, and had devoted himself since that time, according to his own story, in attacking the administration wherever he could. Samuel M. Felker was trying to get the position of Chief of Secret Service away from Washburn, who had succeeded Whitley. Felker had evidently told Wood that he had the promise of the position from Grant. He seemed to think that he could secure favor with the President by being the means of producing evidence favorable to Babcock. This evidence he thought Wood possessed. The letter is a long one. I can only quote certain passages:

Taylor's Hotel, *September* 24, 1876.

Samuel M. Felker, Esq.:

DEAR SAM,—I received your letter of the 21st inst. requesting me to come to Washington at once. . . .

I do not believe you ever received such a promise from the President, and I do not believe you will receive the appointment. Thus I cordially express to you my doubts, because of various delays invented. You now cunningly write me a letter to coax me on to Washington to break up a conspiracy and exonerate General Babcock from all connection with the so-called Safe Burglary, and when the trial is over you will surely be appointed; how easy are promises made—how seldom are they fulfilled—would make a text for the Reverend Doctor Newman. . . . While it is not a matter of commendation, you are fully aware of my ability and intent to do serious damage to the present administration, by aiming at General Babcock and Mr. Luckey in certain matters coming within the range of my aptitude. . . .

I had no special cause for personal attack on General Grant, but as he countenanced the treatment put upon me by Mr. Boutwell . . . personally I believe him to be an honest, conscientious gentleman, and yet feeling the disgrace put upon me by his advisers, I have for years toiled with untiring perseverance to strike at every official act or shortcoming of his subordinates. . . . You have more than once deceived me into a belief that the President would cause your appointment to be made—this was subterfuge—for he would certainly not himself have promised you and then put you off—such are not his characteristics. . . .

You brought Whitley, Washburn (present chief), and myself into one special arrangement. . . . You are aware of the prompt manner I faithfully performed all and more than I conditioned in conjunction with and for the benefit of Mr. Washburn, and how he subsequently, with his low, infamous trickery ever predominating, has yet failed to fill the part which the S. S. Division conditioned with me to perform—instead of which he instituted the most infamous proceedings against George A. Mason, whom he caused to be sent to the Penitentiary after the said Mason had rendered the S. S. Division the most valuable and important service, and in which service he nearly lost his life . . . and Washburn's natural cowardice and dread of Mason incited by the vindictive spirit of this long, slim fellow (Washburn), *who toadied with Wilson as co-laborer and co-plotter against his superiors of the National Administration.* . . . Such examples make me question every movement I may be invited or solicited to entertain. ...

This is the condition, and the only one, on which I will show up the whole of the Safe Burglary conspiracy, and that in such a manner as will *fully and positively exonerate General Babcock from any and all connection with the so-called Safe Burglary,* fully supporting the same with my own evidence, which will fully explode the whole bubble; you are sufficiently aware of the details of the job to know that Whitley himself, although he was the originator and sole schemer in the affair, would not have been suspicioned, *had I not bargained and arranged with Bluford Wilson* (then solicitor) to give that publicity in the *Sun* to the matter which it subsequently received; you can thus infer how complete a vindication of General Babcock can be made with the evidence at my command. . . . W. A. Cook, Esq., tried to glean from me sufficient details to make such a defence as he believed he could do with my assistance and evidence. But he is not possessed with what he wants, and I know the case cannot be properly made up without my evidence and assistance.

I owe the present administration no allegiance, no gratitude, no obligation or reverence, and have it yet in my power to do much damage; there are matters not yet too late for trouble or too private for publicity, which I intended for the Sun. You persuaded me out of that with more of your sophistry, but now Mr. Dana urges me in the most coaxing style for the subject, together with the papers (which are not destroyed as supposed), for which he offers me a very liberal sum ($5000). . . . This letter must not get into the possession of any one—no copy or extract must be taken therefrom.

As ever, your friend,
WM. P. WOOD.

I have wished to call attention to this letter for several reasons. It reveals the part that the Secret Service was playing and had played in the whiskey

POLITICAL DISSENSION

trials and the safe burglary. Bell and Yaryan, who brought testimony to the trial at St. Louis which would have been damaging to Babcock had it not been discredited, were Secret Service men. They had undoubtedly sold their testimony, just as Wood was ready either to sell information to the Sun which would attack Babcock and the administration, or, for some less tangible bribes—probably a position in the Secret Service if Felker succeeded—to furnish testimony which would clear Babcock. It is not wise to believe the statements of such men as these, unless there are other facts to substantiate them. But there are other points which tend to prove that something of what Wood says was true. And I submit it as a clue which other men whose business is historical research may follow up.

Just before the close of President Grant's administration, General Babcock was made Superintendent of the Lighthouse Board, and Mr. Luckey resigned his place as Secretary of Utah to take one under General Babcock. I once went down to Fortress Monroe, where General Babcock had his headquarters, to visit him. He entertained me generously, taking me around in the boats of the Service, and showing me all the sights.

It was a comparatively short time after this that he was drowned. Mr. Luckey was with him. They were just off Key West, where they had sailed on a trip of inspection, when they were overtaken by a storm and went down—together.

I have in my possession the official paper on which

is entered General Babcock's assignment to office as the President's private secretary. It contains also the entry of his application for relief from the assignment, indorsed by General Grant. In addition are these words in General Grant's own handwriting:

> For faithful and efficient service as private secretary for more than six years of my two terms of office, he has my acknowledgment and thanks, and the assurance of my confidence and great efficiency.
>
> U. S. GRANT.

That was the way President Grant was loyal to his friends—there never was a more steadfast man. If it meant nothing more than that he was capable of believing in men in spite of appearances, I would still feel that this trust in Babcock was a fine thing. But I believe that it meant more than this. I have heard it said that General Babcock seemed to cast a spell over the President. Well, then, he cast a spell over me, too. I shall always believe that General Babcock was guilty of nothing worse than of being a friend to men of whose real pursuits he was ignorant.

There was another man to whom General Grant was loyal when it cost him much to be so. That was in the case of General Belknap, the Secretary of War in the second administration. Belknap was a brave man and a good soldier, and as such he had won General Grant's admiration. Up to the time of his fall he was a poor man with an unblemished reputation. He had always stood for an honest man.

His wife was a peculiarly beautiful and fascinating woman, and was the sister of General Belknap's first wife. On her marriage she drew her husband into the full tide of social dissipation. Mrs. Belknap became a conspicuous figure at all the great official functions as well as at everything else that was fashionable and brilliant. The number of her Worth gowns seemed inexhaustible—Worth was the great man dressmaker of that day. Nobody could deny that she seemed made to wear them. She was a handsome woman, with the smallest and prettiest foot in Washington. The Belknaps entertained extravagantly. It might very easily have been wondered how so much luxury was supported on the salary of a Secretary of War.

It was not long before there began to be ugly rumors connecting the Belknap name with the sale of traderships at the military posts. These were lucrative positions, especially where no competition was permitted. When it was clear that he would be impeached, the Secretary of War resigned. It was understood that this was to avoid impeachment. It seemed an admission of guilt, together with a cowardly attempt to escape the consequences. It was wondered why as brave a man as Belknap should have thought of flight, and why the President should have accepted his resignation under the circumstances.

I happened to be present at the final scene. General Belknap was admitted to the President's office. He came forward to the desk and said:

"I have come to offer my resignation, Mr. President." He was a fine, large man, with military carriage and a long patriarchal beard, which was considered a mark of distinction in those days. But now nobody could have helped feeling sorry for him. He looked heartbroken. The President met Belknap's eyes—and there was pity in his:

"I am sorry, Belknap," was all he said. But the two men shook hands.

After the impeachment Belknap practised law in Washington; he had an office on New York Avenue between Thirteenth and Fourteenth streets. I used often to visit him there in the evening. We would sit and smoke for hours together. General Belknap was a kindly, genial man. Mrs. Belknap and her daughter spent much of their time abroad. They were abroad when he died.

In talking about the criticisms made of General Grant's administration, I do not want to give the impression that he himself was unduly depressed by all the abuse. Of course, his decline in popularity was evident to himself as to those by whom he was surrounded. The second administration was a great contrast to the first. But he took it all apparently as one of the fortunes of war. He was stouter, and appeared in better health when he left the White House than when he entered it. During the worst of the attacks on him he never looked worn, as he did when I saw him during the battle of Petersburg. He believed in himself too much to be shaken by abuse. There was a certain quality of his character, a singleness of purpose, which had made him great as a commanding general, that was so absolute as to be

POLITICAL DISSENSION

almost callousness. That was one reason why he was so fond of horse-racing on the road.

One of his races I was concerned in myself. Every one knows of General Grant's fondness for horses. Since his first horse trade, made at the age of eight, he had had an interesting succession of fast steeds. When he was in the White House President Grant always had six horses of his own—sometimes twelve—besides the ponies and other horses belonging to the rest of the family. Cincinnati, who had carried General Grant through the war, was the favorite. Clayborn and Rocky Mountain were the road team, and they could trot to the pole in two-forty. Now, Major Sniffen also possessed a fast mare. I used often to drive with him. One afternoon he decided that we would try to have a race with the President. It was not long before the opportunity presented itself. General Grant started out one afternoon driving Clayborn and Rocky Mountain. He had his youngest boy, Jesse, with him. We followed him. He took the road to Bladensburg. He was almost there when we drove alongside and saluted him:

"I am glad to see you out," he said, with a smile, and a side-glance at the mare. "How far are you going?"

"Only to the spring," said Major Sniffen.

"I am going there myself." When we reached the spring President Grant turned his horses toward home, with a measuring glance at us that meant a race.

The course back to the city was five miles; most of

the time the road was not wide enough to allow two teams abreast. So the President had no difficulty at first in keeping his start. When we came to within a mile and a half of the city we had a wide, level stretch before us. Then Major Sniffen let his horse out. For nearly a mile we were neck to neck and going at a fearful pace for a country road. Then one of the President's horses broke into a run. At that moment Sniffen touched his mare with the whip, and she made a spurt which brought us ahead and won the race.

President Grant took his defeat good-naturedly enough—but the next day he bought the mare. That was characteristic of him.

Of another more reckless race I happened to be a spectator. It was a short time after Major Sniffen's victory. I was driving quietly along the Seventh Street road one evening, when I heard the sharp clatter of hoofs behind me. I pulled to one side—my horse couldn't compete with anything—and then saw that one of the three racers was General Grant. He was driving his trotting - horse. Butcher Boy. His competitors, one on either side of him, had him in a pocket, and evidently did not intend to let him out. But they didn't know their man. I did, and looked out for danger. I knew that Butcher Boy could outclass either of them; and I knew that the President was not apt to stay behind. I can see him now as he leaned forward, bent over the dash-board until his face almost touched it. He had pulled his slouch hat over his forehead until nothing could be seen of

POLITICAL DISSENSION

his face but a grim mouth set as if the lips could never be unlocked, and narrowed eyes gleaming under the hat brim. He smashed straight ahead at his enemies. He was almost on them. From the looks they darted at him, at that instant, they seemed to know—what they ought to have known all the time—that he proposed to pass over them or through them—any way so he passed them. For an instant the outcome was doubtful, for the other fellows looked pretty determined too. I began to shiver. But when Butcher Boy's nose was within an inch of the shoulder of the right-hand man, the man gave way. It was well that he did. The President would have gone straight ahead. He was willing enough to be beaten fairly, but anything like jockeying infuriated him.

It was in the spirit he showed in that race that President Grant conducted his administration. He regretted the discomfiture of those who had been disloyal to him just as much as he would have regretted —had he survived long enough to regret—a smash-up while he was passing those men. He had conducted matters as seemed best to him. He had trusted the men he believed to be trustworthy. In cases where he was convinced they had betrayed him and the country, he dismissed them from his consciousness. Where he was not convinced that a man had been disloyal, he dismissed from his mind, in the same manner, the charges against that man. I don't believe that General Grant ever considered himself responsible for the things that happened. They were incidental to his course.

15

When his course in the White House was approaching its end, and the 4th of March of 1877 drew near, there was much to be done to prepare for the reception of Mr. and Mrs. Hayes. An inventory of household things had to be made, and the effects of General Grant and his family separated from the White House furnishings. Mr. Ulysses S. Grant, Jr., did most of this work. Mrs. Grant went around through all the rooms making her final arrangements, and saying good-bye. It had been a pleasant home for her for eight years, and was endeared by every association. Birth, marriage, and death had come to those nearest to her within the White House walls. I know that she was saddened while she made those last pilgrimages. But she gave thought to the comfort of these who were coming in. Beckley was instructed to order an abundance of provisions so that Mrs. Hayes would not need to concern herself with housekeeping details for some time. The White House store-rooms were well stocked with everything but meats and fresh vegetables. General Grant also gave orders that a selection of the various wines which they had been accustomed to use on their own table should be left in the cellar. He said he did not know whether Mr. and Mrs. Hayes would use them; but the wines would be there if the President-elect and his wife cared for them.

The 4th of March in 1877 came on Sunday, so the inauguration ceremonies were divided between Saturday, the 3d, and the following Monday. On Saturday I accompanied President Grant when he went to the

POLITICAL DISSENSION

Capitol the last time. A steady stream of Congressmen and personal friends and people who wished to ask for last favors passed in and out of the doors of the President's room. There was a hum of conversation, and the room was blue with cigar smoke, A great many men came in just to wring his hand; but there was always a group about his desk of friends who remained for a last chat with President Grant, The mass of bills that are always hurried through the last days of the session had to be brought in and signed. The President, cigar tilted up in mouth, signed, and I blotted. One of the bills that was brought in was to appropriate money to pay the claim of a retired army officer whom I happened to know. It was for $12,000, and would go far to make the old gentleman comfortable. There was a prospect that it would be crowded out, and that would mean that it would possibly never be paid.

Mr. Robeson, Secretary of the Navy, was on the other side of the room. He had the bill on his desk, I went over to him and spoke of the matter:

"I know this man, Mr. Secretary," I said, "and I hope you will recommend the President to sign it. Please don't let the administration go out without this last act of kindness to an old man."

Mr. Robeson examined the bill, and then said:

"All right. Crook. Take it over to the President and tell him I say it's a just claim."

So the President signed it, and I blotted it.

On that same day an elaborate luncheon was served for Mrs. Hayes and the ladies who accompanied her,

But a far more ceremonious affair was the great state dinner at night, at which thirty guests were entertained. President-elect and Mrs. Hayes were, of course, the guests of honor. The cabinet officers and their wives, Senator Sherman, and various other notables were present. Dinner was served at half-past seven. The menu was long and elaborate. General Grant had selected the wines to be served with each course, and had marked them on the menu so there could be no mistake. He was a man who delighted in all the offices of hospitality. I have never known a man who took more interest in the little details by which he could assure himself of the comfort and pleasure of his guests. Everything belonging to good-fellowship and good cheer was dear to him. He enjoyed friends, and he enjoyed friendship. That is one reason why, when misfortune came, he found that there were so many men who loved him. It was in accordance with his character that the usual dinner given by the outgoing to the incoming President should, in the hands of General and Mrs. Grant, have seemed a spontaneous act of generous hospitality.

At twelve o'clock that night, in the first moments of the 4th of March, the oath of office was administered to President Hayes. This was done because, since the 4th fell on Sunday, and the inauguration ceremonies were to be on Monday, there would otherwise have been a day during which, officially, there would have been no Executive. The dinner guests were gathered together in the Red Room, and

POLITICAL DISSENSION

there Chief-Justice Waite swore in the new President. But Mr. and Mrs. Hayes did not remain at the White House that night; they returned to the home of Senator Sherman, where they were being entertained. The next Monday General and Mrs. Grant took their leave, and President and Mrs. Hayes moved in.

The real farewell of most of the White House employees to General Grant was on the afternoon of the 3d, when he left the Executive Mansion to go to the Capitol. It was a characteristic one, too. A number of his friends had gathered at the White House, so quite a little company followed him out to the portico to see him start off. I stood ready to accompany him. Everybody felt pretty sad. He had been kind to us all. One after another, the •men pressed forward to shake his hand. He started toward the steps. Some one in the crowd called out the usual trite remark: "Well, Mr. President, this is your last day!" General Grant turned at the head of the steps: "Well," he replied, slowly, "I can't say as my illustrious predecessor did"—here he smiled a little— "that I go out with the approval of the whole country. I know I don't. And I believe I'm glad of it!"

Then he turned again and walked down the steps with his quick, decided walk, and his square shoulders set.

XII

RUTHERFORD B. HAYES IN THE WHITE HOUSE

THE very first official act of President Hayes put all of us of the White House staff at our ease. At that time there was always more or less anxiety among the executive clerks, as in all the departments, at the beginning of each administration, for fear the incoming President might want our places for his own friends. It might be weeks or months before we felt safe, but in the case of President Hayes we did not have long to wait. The afternoon of Inauguration Day we were all sitting quietly at our desks, with suspense in the air. I had just settled myself after catching a glimpse of Mrs. Hayes in the corridor, with her little nine-year-old daughter Fanny, inspecting her new domain. In passing she gave me a pleasant glance from her lustrous brown eyes. I turned to look after her, and noticed how gracefully she walked. But at that moment we were wondering when the President would come in.

There was a little stir as a quiet, solidly built man with a fine full beard entered. Grant has said of Hayes: "His conduct on the field was marked by conspicuous gallantry, as well as the display of qualities of a higher order than mere personal daring."

R. B. HAYES IN THE WHITE HOUSE

While there was a complete absence of military swagger, President Hayes carried himself with soldierly uprightness.

I rose at my desk, but he had crossed the floor before I could meet him, and shook my hand with the cordiality that we all afterward grew to expect from him.

"What are your duties, Mr. Crook?" he asked.

I explained as well as I could in a few words.

"Well," he said, "just continue to perform your duties. You will not be disturbed."

I went home that night feeling that the new President was going to be a good man to work for.

Other men in the office were sure of it, and with reason. Mr. C. C. Sniffen, who had been assistant private secretary in Grant's second administration, was promoted to be major and paymaster in the army. Mr. O. L. Pruden, a clerk in the office, was made, through the friendship of Major Sniffen, assistant private secretary. The secretary was Mr. Rogers, formerly an Episcopal clergyman. He was an admirable, kindly man, but had little executive ability. There were minor changes: a few new clerks were appointed, the telephone and telegraph services were introduced. By-the-way, it is surprising how up to date this made us feel. Previous to this, there had been a great deal of talk about Civil-Service Reform, while very little had been actually accomplished. But now the principles that had been in the air were brought down to earth—in the Executive Office. In a few days a new feeling began to pervade it. We realized that there would be recognition of faithful service. The sharp distinctions that had been made between certain positions were gone. Somehow, we were all men of much the same class, working together on an equality.

Among the changes in the office there was one interesting feature thoroughly in keeping with the character of the President and with the whole administration. A stenographer, G. A. Gustin, sat always in the President's office. When one realizes that nothing could be said to the President, nor could he say anything, except in the presence of a third person, a man begins to wonder how much of the character of the administration was due to this fact. It also becomes evident what sort of man it was who preferred to have state affairs public.

There were no cabinet quarrels, so far as was known, nor was there any jealousy. Secretaries Evarts, Sherman, and Schurz were at the White House more than the others and seemed to have most influence.

Mrs. Hayes managed her domestic affairs with the same ease and smoothness that her husband did his cabinet. She followed the same method, too, of placing authority in the hands of those she could trust. Winnie Monroe, the cook—a fat old woman who was as black as a crow—came with Mrs. Hayes from Ohio, and W. T. Crump, the steward, followed in a few weeks. Both Winnie and Crump were devoted to their employers—Winnie adored Mrs. Hayes. So they looked out for the interests of the President

RUTHERFORD B. HAYES

R. B. HAYES IN THE WHITE HOUSE

and his wife, and at the same time kept everything as peaceful as possible. In my recollection there never has been a time when the White House was so well served. It was such a glorious period for Winnie that she was not at all contented when, with the Hayes family, she retired to Ohio and private life. She soon was back in Washington:

"Law, chile," she remarked to one of her fellow-officials who had remained in the White House service, "I cain't stay in no Ohio—not aftah I been fu'st culled lady in de lan'!" It is fortunate that the daughter of the "fu'st culled lady" had secured a Government position. That the maintenance of social position had proved expensive is proved by the fact that when Winnie died, not long afterward, the daughter sent to General Hayes for help. The General telegraphed me from Ohio to make all the necessary funeral arrangements and send the bill to him.

Crump, the steward, told me of an incident that showed how fastidious President Hayes was about some things. It had been the custom during the Grant administration to buy the groceries of the army commissary. This was perfectly natural and proper, because of the army associations of General Grant. At the commissary the very best things were to be obtained at cost price. This President Hayes refused to do. "I prefer to buy like other men," he said.

The peacefulness that reigned in the cabinet-room and offices, and that permeated the kitchen and pantry, was a sort of reflection of the peace and order that filled the big square rooms in the President's private apartments and brooded over the corridor. The Hayes family was an affectionate and harmonious one. To begin with, the President was genial and even-tempered. Mrs. Hayes would have been considered an unusual woman wherever placed. People were always saying that she was a clever woman. One would know, from the way she carried herself and from her face, that she was a woman of much character; the deference shown her by her husband would have proved it if nothing else did. But her cleverness was not what most impressed White House employees. What we felt was her sweetness, her kindness, and the sunniness of her disposition. She was a bright, happy woman.

The executive ability of the President's wife was shown to great advantage in the troublesome matter of refurnishing the White House, with no money with which to do it. Because of the political situation Congress had failed to make an appropriation. Yet, when the Grants left, the place was in the state of shabbiness that usually marked the end of an administration. Mrs. Hayes ransacked attic and cellar to find furniture that had been stored away for years and, in some cases, forgotten. Many really good things owed their preservation to this energetic lady.

She took pride in keeping up the historical associations of the mansion. I am sure the only piece of lobbying that she ever did was undertaken to get possession, for the White House, of the Martha Washington portrait. She invited the proper Congressmen to dinner, and after that function profifered her request with a smile from bright and pretty eyes. And she got what she wanted. In this case, however, not even President Hayes could criticise; for it was due to him that the White House collection of portraits was made fairly complete. He made this project one of his pursuits. He also had the library catalogued.

It was quite in keeping that she should have loved flowers as she did. The White House conservatories had never been the object of so much interest on the part of the mistress as during her time. She brought from Ohio Henry Pfister, the florist, who was in his element. By her wishes the billiard-room that used to connect the conservatories with the house was made into a conservatory, the billiard - table being moved into the basement. A rose house and a violet house were constructed and long-closed windows were opened that guests seated at a state dinner could look through long vistas in the conservatory.

These additions were necessary to supply all the flowers Mrs. Hayes wanted to give away, for that was the chief use she made of them. Flowers went from her to the Children's Hospital almost every day; anything that helped children appealed to her more than other charities. Whenever a friend was ill, flowers were sent to the sick - room; White House employees, home on sick-leave, received them every day. Her love for flowers was as distinctive as her dress.

During the four years that Mrs. Hayes held social

sway, she was never influenced to change in any detail her manner of dressing her hair. She always wore rich materials; taste then ran to heavy, rich fabrics rather than to flimsier things. She never wore a low-necked gown; although her evening costumes might be cut out at the neck in the shape of a heart or a V, it was only to be filled in with some fluffy, filmy stuff. She wore little jewelry unless it were something like the high silver comb of which she was so fond, or the cameo portrait of the President set with diamonds, which she had had made as a souvenir of her silver wedding, which happened the first winter she was in the White House.

Mrs. Hayes was fond of heavy, lustrous white stuffs. Of all flowers she loved best to wear white camellias. With one of these creamy, waxen, perfect things at her breast, and another in her dark hair, with the rose-geranium leaves that she liked about them, she felt that her costume was elaborate enough. Sometimes, when the camellias had all been given away, she wore, instead, a white rosebud. Her hair was so dark a brown that it seemed black. It was wonderfully heavy, and she always wore it looped over her ears in shining bands. With these rich, smooth surfaces, her broad, white forehead, and her large, brown, brilliant eyes, Mrs. Hayes was always conspicuous in a crowd of women.

The fact is, Mrs. Hayes was a handsome woman. It is true that her charm of manner and grace of movement would have made her noticeable anywhere. She had, too, the sort of tact that comes

R. B. HAYES IN THE WHITE HOUSE

from a desire to make people happy, and the influence over others that made them do what she wished without their knowing that they were being influenced.

The Hayes children had many of the traits of both father and mother. Burchard Hayes, the eldest son, did not live in Washington. He was here only for occasional visits, so Webb, the next son, was his father's right-hand man, and attended to his father's personal affairs. I used to see a good deal of Webb Hayes. We often went gunning together after office hours. He was a square, honest fellow. Indeed, all of the boys were, but as Rutherford was away at college most of the time, the White House saw more of Webb and of Scott, the youngest child, than of the other sons. Scott was full of fun and mischief. He used to get into a good deal of trouble because he was pretty—well—enterprising, but he was a nice little fellow all the same.

Fanny, the one daughter and the next to the youngest child, was the pet of the White House. She was attractive, with a perfect complexion and a bright face. Her hair was brown and her eyes were a pretty blue. She used to come into the office to ask me for paper, or something of the sort. Then she would scribble notes to me. I have some of them tucked away. One of them has on the outside, in very straggling letters, the caution," Private," with my name and address. In the corner she has commented, "Very bad writing." All this was the prelude to saying:

> Dear Sir,—I thank you very much for the paper you gave me.
> FANNY.

Another card, which is addressed to "Mr. Crook, Esq.," is in another mood. She says:

> I am *very very very* mad because you have not got large enough book to press my flowers in.

This was when Fanny was eleven years old. Another is formal and legal in tone. I have forgotten what it was that she was referring to—something that the child thought was a joke, I suppose.

> *Mr. Crook:*
> Dear Sir,—I have heard you were not very prompt in paying a poor mian a debt you owed him. I will therefore demand payment *instantly.*
> Very truly,
> F. R. HAYES.

The scraps of writing bring back the picture to me of the merry, busy child running in and out on her own affairs.

Children, as we all know, are usually democratic; but in this case they were reflecting the character of their elders. One incident that I remember shows how simple Mrs. Hayes was. A number of visiting ladies called one morning by appointment. They were not personal friends; they were merely travellers who had come to Washington from a distance. Mrs. Hayes showed them all through the private apartments; she knew that these matrons from the Middle West would be interested in White House housekeeping more than in both Houses of Congress and the Supreme Court combined. The ladies afterward reported, with approbation, that "everything was in order at nine o'clock in the morning." You may be sure they told in their home towns that Mrs. Hayes was a good housekeeper.

One of the prettiest things that happened at the White House while I was there had Mrs. Hayes for its chief actor I suppose it might have been embarrassing to another kind of woman. A veteran of the War of 1812 was to have his photograph taken at the White House. The old fellow lived at the Soldiers' Home, but the brand-new uniform ordered for the occasion had been sent direct to the Executive Mansion. When Mrs. Hayes discovered him he was almost tearful with grief because the sergeant's stripes that marked his rank had not been sewed on, but had been placed beside his clothes in the paper box. Mrs. Hayes whipped out her housewife in an instant, placed the now smiling veteran on a divan in the Blue Room, and was sitting on the floor in front of him, busily stitching on his stripes, when Sir Edward Thornton, the British Minister, with some English friends whom he wished to present to the President's wife, was ushered into the room! It is not wonderful that all of the troops of her husband's regiment, and any others who had known her* adored Mrs. Hayes. And just as when, a handsome young matron of thirty, she started out to find her wounded husband at the front, she encountered nothing but helpfulness along the almost impassable road from Ohio to the military hospital, so she usually had her own kindly way with any soldier whom she met. For they were all to her like the wounded "boys" she had nursed in hospital or heartened upon the field.

President Hayes, on his part, had a kindly fashion of speaking of the clerks and secretaries in the Executive Office as "my office family." When one of us was standing by him and some one else came up, he always presented us. This may not have been rigidly official, but it did make one feel like a human being. Both President and Mrs. Hayes introduced pleasant customs for the benefit of the "office family" of which I shall speak later on. One of the smaller outings in which I was usually included was when the President and his wife went out to Rock Creek to shoot at a target. Sometimes Fanny and Scott would be with us. We would drive up Fourteenth Street to the Rock Creek Road. Straight down the road, in a particularly lovely spot, was a big birch-tree that overlooked the water. On this I would hang the target, and we would all try our skill. Sometimes the children would want a shot, too, but one trial would content them, and they would run off to find other amusement. The President hit the bull's-eye five times out of six, but neither Mrs. Hayes nor I was so good a shot.

It was the happy time of the department clerks, also, though probably none of them would have admitted it. But it wasn't the happy time of Senators and Members and political bosses who couldn't get the "patronage" they thought they were entitled to. During the early days of the Hayes administration the question was whether the President would really carry out the principles of Civil-Service Reform. From his letter of acceptance, of course, he was pledged to it; he had been identified with the movement before he became a candidate; but those of us who had stood between past Presidents and the daily hordes of office-seekers were doubtful whether it would be possible for any one man to withstand the pressure.

To a large extent President Hayes did withstand the pressure. I can state, from my personal acquaintance with clerks in the different departments, that, so far as displacements were concerned, the Civil-Service Reform principles were carried out. The President also attempted to prevent applications for positions being made to him in person. Instructions were published in the newspapers and posted at the White House stating that applications should be made in writing and submitted to the proper head of department. I remember that the President said:

"It is an imposition that such things should take up so much of the time of the President of the United States!"

Practically these instructions were not observed to any great extent. The President was too kindly a man not to be accessible to those who wanted to see him.

The great thing that was done—and that was the point on which the President worked in harmony with his Secretary of the Interior, Carl Schurz, whom every-body knew to be in earnest about Civil-Service Re-form'— was in establishing competitive examinations for the various offices of the Interior Department. It came to be quite the usual thing to read an announcement in the paper that an examination would be held in the Patent Office or Pension Office or Indian Bureau to determine who would be eligible to fill vacancies in those departments. The Post-Office Department also tried the method, but more rarely. It is well known that the President also insisted upon Civil-Service Reform in the New York Custom House and Post-Office.

There was one very necessary reform that the President carried through—for all time, I believe. There had been a kind of political blackmail going on in the departments. The campaign managers virtually had been levying on the clerks large contributions to the Republican campaign fund, the clerks being afraid not to give the money. The President was indignant over this abuse. He had orders circulated in the departments to the effect that clerks were not to be required to make such contributions, nor were Government officials to take a prominent part in party organizations. Government employees might go home to vote, but they were to have no part in State party organizations.

His attitude on the second-term question was another example of the same thing. He had announced at the time of his election that in no circumstances would he accept a renomination. He was opposed to the idea on principle. Now, men have held that theory who, after a taste of power, have been led to change their minds. But Rutherford B. Hayes was never influenced in the least. No action while he was in the White House was aimed at popularity. Everything that he did was done because, according to his own principles, it was right. I have heard President Hayes say:

"I believe the second-term idea is opposed to the principles of Republican government."

Moreover, I believe that throughout his life Hayes preferred private to public life. Before he was nominated for the Presidency he had shown that preference. In 1872, when the nomination for Congress was offered to him, he at first refused, and he was led to accept only when he was convinced his acceptance was for the good of the party. When he left the White House it was with the intention not to return to public life. In a letter written to me December 23, 1888, he said: "Of course all rumors about my taking any place, etc., etc., are untrue."

Another promise made in his letter of acceptance which was unpopular with many of the Republican Party and which he still persisted in carrying out, was that with regard to removing the Federal troops from the South. There was an interesting story told by a newspaper correspondent at the time to explain how General Hayes had come to this decision. I cannot vouch for it, of course, but it is certainly characteristic of the man as I knew him.

The correspondent asked President Hayes why he had decided to withdraw the troops from the South:

"Well," said the President, "while I was thinking about my letter of acceptance and what would be my policy when President, I began to ponder on the state of almost anarchy in the South. I said to myself: 'These Southerners are men like the rest of us. They are neither cut-throats nor bandits; they are average men. There must be some reason why neighbor is killing neighbor down there, why they are violating the national law, some reason outside of themselves, for the rest of Americans are living in peace and order.'

"Then the battle of the Antietam campaign came into my mind. I remembered that, as I stood watching the slaughter—men cut down in swaths—I had rejoiced at it, been glad to see a thing at which, at another time, I should have shuddered—

"'It was because it was war that we all loved violence at that time,' I said to myself. 'And now, it is because they feel that they are still living in a state of war that the Southern men are killing one another. It is the presence of the troops that keeps the strife alive.' And at that moment I made up my mind that when I became President I would withdraw the troops."

And withdraw them he did, in spite of the displeasure of many of the leaders of the party who feared that the President's action would lose the Republicans votes in the South. That action of President Hayes was the beginning of real peace; from it dated a revival of industries which became possible only when North and South again co-operated in the Government.

Still a third point of the President's policy he

R. B. HAYES IN THE WHITE HOUSE

maintained in opposition to his party. In this he acted in accordance with the Secretary of the Treasury, John Sherman. Both men were determined to fight for sound money; and when President Hayes vetoed the Silver Coinage Act he knew he was doing an unpopular thing. But he vetoed it just the same. The bill was passed over his veto.

The calmness with which he received the news of the defeat of his policy in this matter made clear a trait of the President's character that was as marked as his firmness. He was a calm, reasoning man, in earnest, but not passionately so. The night the Silver Coinage passed over his veto there happened to be a state dinner. The veto of the bill and its passage were topics that made table-talk. There was a good deal of facetious conversation about it, in which the President took part—in fact he was rather merry in his genial way. It was not that he hid his disappointment as a sportsmanlike thing to do; he was really satisfied with doing his part under the Constitution and with having registered his opinion about the thing. Imagine Andrew Johnson, or any other good fighter, being reasonably calm and satisfied to have a measure pass which he honestly thought was bad for the country!

I suppose it was because both he and Mrs. Hayes came to be known as unprejudiced and interested in reforms that the White House became the resort of everybody with a grievance or a theory. It was well the President and his wife were interested in educational, moral, and religious matters; they must have had their fill of them while they were in Washington. Every question that had been put aside, waiting for the country to be really at peace again, came up for discussion.

Early in the administration the Indian troubles came to a head. There was delegation upon delegation of Indians who had come—in war-paint and blankets—to see the Great Father. Sitting Bull came first with his followers; then the Poncas. The Sioux followed, but they had left their native dress and their war-paint at home and wore American clothes. It became quite the ordinary thing to see groups of braves stalking into the President's office for a conference. The meeting between the President and the chiefs was something to remember. Each brave had an opportunity of making a speech:

"We are a little people," said one. "We are being driven into the sea."

" We want to remain on the lands our fathers had; we want our children to be educated and to live like white men, but we do not want to be driven into the lands where there is no water."

"I was foolish at first," said one old fighter, "but I know more now. I will not put on my war bonnet again to go forth against the white men."

The burden of every speech was a plea against further seizure of their lands. They were sent home with presents and promises. The promises were kept, moreover, for President Hayes's administration was the beginning of a more just and humane policy toward the Indians.

R. B. HAYES IN THE WHITE HOUSE

The women suffragists, too, were much in evidence, Mrs. Hayes was, of course, the object of their special interest. She received them graciously and sweetly. I do not know how she felt about it, but I wonder if the place she occupied in the President's life and in the minds of her four boys might not have been as much power as any one woman would have wanted to have. Every one remembers President Hayes's remark to a Western delegation:

"I don't know how much influence Mrs. Hayes has with Congress, but she has great influence with me."

While he was still in the White House the main feature of the social reform work of himself and Mrs. Hayes—somehow it seems natural to speak of them together, they were so united in everything—was in connection with the temperance movement. We knew of their convictions before they took possession, and were all wondering whether they would or would not have wine served at official entertainments. We were not long left in doubt as to Mrs. Hayes's preference in the matter.

When the two young Russian grand-dukes, Alexis and Constantine, visited Washington there was much excitement. "Would Mrs. Hayes have wine at the dinner in their honor? And if she did not, what would Alexis and Constantine and Russia and the whole civilized world think about us?" The dinner was to be on the 19th of April. Before that time Mr. Evarts came to the relief of the situation. Being Secretary of State, of course the matter came within his province; and he was not only a clever man, but more respectful of forms than many other leaders in public life. I remember that he was the first gentleman in Washington to wear a frock-coat at the New-Year's reception at the White House. Up to that time every caller had presented himself, at eleven in the morning, in a dress-suit. But, about the wine: Mr. Evarts said that, since the Russian grand-dukes were accustomed to have it served at dinner, it would be a failure to entertain them properly, and consequently a lack of respect to Russia, if there were no wine. So it was served, although the glasses in front of the President and his wife were untouched, and the noble guests partook without realizing the excitement they had caused. I believe there would have been no serious complications if the debated beverage had been absent; the visitors were both too young to be punctilious. They were tall, well-set-up young men, Alexis noticeably so, and in general not unlike Americans in appearance.

They say that Mrs. Hayes was afterward sorry that she had done violence to her convictions in the matter. For a time the temperance organizations were indignant with her. But, as it was the first, it was also the last time that anything alcoholic was served at dinner while Mrs. Hayes was in the White House. So the temperance organizations forgave her, and soon they began to worship her. All of the societies in the country united to have a portrait painted of her which should remain in the White House. This was done while she was in Washington. The artist

R. B. HAYES IN THE WHITE HOUSE

was Daniel Huntington, and he succeeded in painting a splendid likeness, which hangs in one of the corridors of the White House. Then the Cincinnati School of Design presented a heavily carved oak frame for the picture. It was a handsome thing in itself, but it was not specially effective for the purpose for which it was designed: it did not set off the picture. During a later administration this frame was removed, and a heavy gilt one was substituted. Then there was a commotion about that. The temperance societies felt that proper respect had not been paid to them or the frame. They wrote to the White House about it, requesting that the frame be rescued and sent to the National Museum. Before anything was done about it, however. General Hayes wrote to me, from Fremont, Ohio, on the 3d of December, 1887:

> My dear Colonel,—Some ladies who are on the Committee of the Ohio Centennial to prepare an exhibit of Woman's Work, and who were also connected with the Committee who presented the carved frame of the Huntington portrait of Mrs. Hayes, wish to know if they can have the frame returned for the Centennial.
>
> Old articles are sometimes sold at auction, when no longer of use at the Executive Mansion. If anything of this kind is done, please bid it off in your name, or in some other, and I will send you the funds and return it to the ladies or the party by whom it was given, I hope, of course, to return it without a sale....
>
> Sincerely,
> RUTHERFORD B. HAYES.

With a note which I received from General Hayes some months later, the incident was closed:

THROUGH FIVE ADMINISTRATIONS

Fremont, O., 13 *April,* 1888.

My dear Friend,—Your note of the 6th came during my Centennial trip to Marietta. I have just seen it, having returned only last night. I am more than mortified that I did not write thanking you for your good friendly work as to the frame. It was duly received by President Merrick— a suitable, quiet, newspaper paragraph prepared by him— and all are happy. I am exceedingly obliged. Mrs. Hayes manifested more gratification than I anticipated when she found it was safely back with the givers. We are specially your debtors, and the President's.

By-the-way, he delighted us greatly by the appointment of your namesake. General Crook.

With all friendship. *Come to see us* any time, except when we are away from home.

Sincerely,
RUTHERFORD B. HAYES.

Just a short time ago an incident occurred, suggested probably by the affair of the frame, that shows what absurd misunderstandings arise when the papers are particularly in need of news. A wail went up all over the country because a heavily carved sideboard, presented to Mrs. Hayes by the young ladies of the Cincinnati School of Design, had been sold at auction and was adorning some saloon in the city. As a matter of fact President Hayes would not permit presents to Mrs. Hayes, but it was purchased by Colonel Casey, Superintendent of Public Buildings and Grounds, for the White House, although known as the Hayes sideboard. It was furnished under contract by a Cincinnati firm in 1880. When the White House was remodelled during the present administration, according to an old precedent, such furniture as was not in keeping with the new plans was sold,

R. B. HAYES IN THE WHITE HOUSE

Because of the attitude of President and Mrs. Hayes toward the temperance movement, a large element in the country thought them both narrow-minded fanatics. But there was nothing fanatical about them. Beyond the one instance of the stand with regard to their own table at the White House, they made no effort to interfere in the affairs of others. They could be genial and companionable without being untrue to their principles. They were hospitable and loved to put their best before friends. Although the President did not smoke, there was rarely a time when they did not have cigars for their guests.

The trip to Richmond the autumn after the inauguration was another case in point. The railroad company spared no expense on the special car. The dinner was elaborate, and there were both whiskey and wine on the table. Neither the President nor Mrs. Hayes made objection to any one in the party drinking as much as he saw fit. Of course their glasses were turned down. Otherwise, they made no sign of their opinions. In this case the responsibility was not theirs, as the Southern Railroad was host.

That was a wonderful thing, when one thinks of it, the Presidential party at the Richmond fair. For the first time since the war, a President, elected by Republicans, united with the South to celebrate the reawakening of industry in that section.

It was a wonderful thing to me, too, who was with them. We went luxuriously; there was a jolly party; there were placid, comfortable faces all about me.

There was no thought of anything but good fellowship and good feeling; yet all the time, as we drew near to Richmond, the thought of the first time I had been there was in my mind, the day, nearly twelve years before, when I was one who entered into Richmond with Lincoln. Then we were a few men in a little boat, dodging the wreckage in the James River. Before us was a burning town, filled with people who hated us; and each time I looked up, there was the pain in Lincoln's face.

But when we got there—President Hayes and his party, I mean, on that October day of 1877—the other time faded from my mind. The crowds who welcomed the President were jubilant, and they made a great deal of noise. The speech he made at the fair was cheered manfully. The holiday spirit took possession of us all. Webb Hayes and I remained after the President and the rest of the party had gone home. We were invited by Capt. John S. Wise, of the Richmond Blues, to go gunning for birds. Webb Hayes was the one of the President's sons who cared most for an active, adventurous life. Much of his father's military instinct had descended to him. Why, just the other day—in 1898—I went down-town, in Washington, with Webb Hayes to help him select his outfit as major of an Ohio cavalry regiment of volunteers in Cuba and Porto Rico. He went to the Philippines and China as a lieutenant. He was colonel before he got back.

XIII

SOCIAL LIFE IN THE HAYES ADMINISTRATION

THERE was a great deal of entertaining at the White House during President Hayes's term. I was certainly in a position to know about expenditures, and I can state that the administration was as lavish as any of its predecessors that I knew anything about, and more so than some that have followed. A single reception cost $3000, and that was only one of a succession of events. There was the usual series of state dinners; Mrs. Hayes gave a great many luncheons for ladies; and the President entertained his cabinet at a number of luncheons. President and Mrs. Hayes never seemed tired of entertaining. When some one asked Mrs. Hayes if the pressure of social duties did not tire her, she said simply:

"Why, I never get tired of having a good time." A great many things conspired to make the administration an unusually interesting one socially. In the first place, besides the official functions, there was a succession of more homely entertainments. The family rarely sat down to dinner without guests. Mrs. Hayes had a number of young ladies with her, who added much to the gayety of the White House; friends who happened to be in conversation with any of the family at the time were invited informally to luncheon. Hardly a week went by that I was not asked to luncheon two or three times, and I, of course, was one of many, I would be consulting Mrs. Hayes about some matter when the meal was announced. Then she would say:

"Won't you come in to lunch with me, Mr. Crook, and we shall have time to talk this over?"

The first December that the Hayeses spent in the White House was marked by a particularly interesting event. The 30th, which came on Sunday, was the twenty-fifth anniversary of the marriage of the President and his wife, and on the 31st there was a silver-wedding reception. Mrs. Hayes stood under a floral wedding bell and wore a gown of heavy white silk, the neck cut heart-shaped and filled in with white illusion. It was at first reported to be the dress she had worn at her wedding, but that was a mistake. It happened that she did wear her real wedding-dress the day before—the real anniversary. It was a quaint gown, the yellowed tints and scant folds of which looked odd enough in that day of draped and elaborate skirts. That quiet family gathering on the 30th was an interesting occasion to those who knew about it. The old minister who had performed the marriage ceremony was present and made some simple, affecting remarks. The child of Mrs. Hayes's friend, Mrs. Herron, was christened, as were also the two White House children, Fanny and Scott.

The wedding of Miss Emily Piatt, who had been

SOCIAL LIFE IN HAYES ADMINISTRATION

one of Mrs. Hayes's assistants during the first social season, was another occasion in which the family circle and more intimate friends were interested. The ceremony was performed in the White House. The groom was General Hastings. It was a very quiet affair, but the Marine Band played, and there were flowers everywhere, as one would have expected in anything with which Mrs. Hayes had to do.

As soon as these more intimate affairs were a feature of the past, the social organization of the administration was undertaken. Mrs. Hayes had certain well-defined principles, and these determined, to a great extent, the social customs of the period. For example, she hated to hurt any one's feelings, and she knew that any discrimination in social preferment is sure to create heart-burnings. Consequently she established forms which were never broken through. At her first afternoon reception of the season, the wives of all the cabinet officers received with her. After that, singly, in fixed order, they assisted at the remaining receptions. With the cabinet lady, Mrs. Hayes's house guests were the only ladies "in line," until the last reception, when all the cabinet ladies were again present. No outside guests were invited to the state dinners. In every way she attempted to make the official social life representative of the country at large, rather than of a privileged class. I think that, to an astonishing degree, she was successful in making the period both dignified and harmonious.

In the official and diplomatic circles certain things

happened to show that Washington was becoming a more important social centre. Of the visit of the Russian grand-dukes I have already spoken. The arrival of the Chinese Minister was another important and picturesque event. At the first reception at which he appeared the newest beauty was eclipsed. The gorgeousness of his costume brought the East into the new country. He wore a pagoda hat with a scarlet plume floating behind it, secured by a jewelled button. His robe was in two shades of lavender silk and scarlet velvet. The ladies looked with envy at his costume and his jewels.

The Earl of Dufferin, a much plainer personage than the Chinese Minister, followed the example of the Russian grand-dukes in paying Washington a visit. He was entertained at a dinner, at which there was no wine. The arrival of General and Mrs. Grant in Washington was the signal for so much entertaining that it almost ranked with a great diplomatic event. The popularity of General Grant was increasing every day. There was a great dinner in their honor at the White House.

One innovation of President and Mrs. Hayes had a lasting effect on the social customs of Washington, the sending out of cards for the great reception to the Diplomatic Corps. From it has grown the series of receptions to the Diplomatic Corps, the Army and Navy, the Judiciary, and Congress, which are perhaps the most important general social events of the season. The first of these receptions was in February, 1878. The indiscriminate evening receptions

SOCIAL LIFE IN HAYES ADMINISTRATION

at the White House had been for many years a source of great annoyance. In Lincoln's time they had been marked by disgraceful vandalism; even when that was not true, there were violations of what one would think the simplest rules of good breeding. Carelessly dressed women who had not even taken the trouble to smooth their hair or wash their faces elbowed—sometimes sharply—women in dainty evening gowns. Sleepy children were dragged into the crush. Cloaks which were often greasy with dirt were worn into the very presence of the receiving party. It had become evident that the time for being democratic was not at evening receptions. Tourists and the curious generally could shake the hand of the President in the afternoon. It was necessary to have some more dignified forms for evening entertainment.

The President and Mrs. Hayes consulted with Secretary Evarts, who had a great deal of influence over the administration in social matters as well as in affairs of state. I have among my papers memoranda in his handwriting for use in White House entertaining. On this occasion they decided to send out invitations for a reception to the Diplomatic Corps. The Senators and Members of Congress, the Army and Navy, the Judiciary, and all higher officials were invited.

The reception made up for any deficiencies in the hastily engraved cards. There were about a thousand guests—I know there was that number at the last reception of the Hayes administration, and I think this one could not have fallen far short. The White House was beautifully decorated, and the refreshments were unusual when one considered how many there were to enjoy them. It seemed to me that nothing was wanting. The state dining-room and the family dining-room were used; and some of the up-stairs rooms, the library, and the offices were utilized as little refreshment-rooms, and here were served terrapin, sweetbreads, bouillon, patties, salads, cream and ices, cakes, coffee, sweetmeats in variety—everything that is possible for a buffet supper except the forbidden wines and punches.

Mrs. Hayes always had a peculiar fondness for girls. She loved to surround herself with young and pretty faces. There were always young women guests at the White House, sometimes relatives, sometimes friends or the daughters of old friends. The number of luncheons for women, young and old, and the lovely spirit of sunny friendliness prevalent at them, made Mrs. Hayes's reign one long to be remembered. The culminating feature of it all was a great luncheon given by the President's wife in the last year of the administration to her seven house guests. Among the fifty women invited to meet her friends were many who have since become prominent in the social, political, and diplomatic life of the nation.

Every Thanksgiving Day the President and Mrs. Hayes gave a dinner to the secretaries and clerks and their families, carrying out the true spirit of the day by making it an occasion for the children. The President used to call the gathering "my office family

SOCIAL LIFE IN HAYES ADMINISTRATION

Reunion." Dinner was served early in the evening, so that the little ones could come. There were place-cards for each and souvenirs for the children. The dinner was as elaborately served as the most ceremonious of the state dinners. Each year President Hayes took in a different lady. The last Thanksgiving of his term it was my wife to whom he gave his arm.

After dinner every one gathered in the Red Parlor, and Mrs. Hayes played games with the children— pussy wants a comer, pass the button, and the like, Fanny and Scott joining in. At last all, about twenty-five in the company, drifted about the piano. Mrs. Hayes played, and we all sang hymns together —sweet old Methodist tunes, for the President and his wife were identified with the old Foundry Church. I suppose some persons would feel inclined to smile at the simplicity of it all; but not any one who was there.

I do not know whether Thanksgiving or Christmas was better. At Christmas-time Mrs. Hayes had a present for every one of the household, secretaries, clerks, doorkeepers. Sometimes she bought the presents herself, in which case she would be at work for weeks beforehand. Sometimes, when she was rushed, she commissioned Webb Hayes and me to buy them. At those times there would be a card for each one, to give the more personal touch. At about noon on Christmas Day every one was called into the library. There, in a heap in the middle of the floor, were the presents. Beside them waited President and Mrs.

Hayes, and little Miss Fanny and Scott waited "first on one foot and then on t'other" for the festivities to begin. The President or his wife read out the names and picked out the presents, and the two children danced about distributing them. I remember my gift the first year was a fine plated silver water-pitcher, which I am still using. It was a real Christmas that came to the White House in those days, and Mrs. Hayes's smile was better than eggnog.

Mr. Webb Hayes was the originator of a method of making a sort of social history of the administration. Maj. O. L. Pruden, of the White House staff, was directed to keep in a bound volume a list of entertainments and guests. Major Pruden, having a pen the cleverness of which he himself had not suspected, began to enter details in ornamental type. Under the encouragement of Mr. Webb Hayes, he became more ambitious in his artistic effects. Finally, each page was made brilliant by elaborate devices of line and color. Scrolls, wreaths of flowers, foliage, pictured wedding bells, flags, coats of arms and pennants, and the names of guests and entertainers, entered in fine and exact penmanship, make the Hayes's "Social Register," now in the possession of Maj. Webb Hayes, a unique volume.

The last months of the Hayes administration was marked by a great number of brilliant functions, including, on the 15th of December, the great dinner to ex-President and Mrs. Grant; and in February a dinner to the trustees of the Peabody Educational Fund. There was also a dinner to Mrs. John Jacob

SOCIAL LIFE IN HAYES ADMINISTRATION

Astor, and the luncheon to the young ladies already mentioned. Major Pruden had outdone himself in the elaboration of his artistic effects. He adapted his color scheme and floral effects to the case in hand. The young ladies were fitly celebrated in wreaths of pink rosebuds; the great banquet to the President-elect and Mrs. Garfield on the 3d of March was made brave by many a device in which the flag and the national colors played their part. It was at that dinner, by-the-way, that youth and age met in a friendly and sympathetic fashion. For "Grandma Garfield," being unequal to a whole evening of state dining, retired early, and Miss Fanny Hayes had her first experience with the splendors of an official banquet. For an hour or so Mrs. Hayes let her little daughter take Grandma Garfield's place at table.

But it all had to come to an end. Only two months after that last Christmas, and it was Inauguration Day again. I was driving with President Hayes to the Capitol for the last time. He went there to sign any bills that might be waiting for his signature. As it happened, there was none ready; so he told the coachman to drive to the Riggs Hotel for General Garfield. In the quiet of the carriage he turned to me and said:

"I didn't have time to say what I wanted to to the rest. Will you take a message for me?"

"Indeed I will, Mr. President," I said.

"Say to every one connected with my office," he said, "that I want them to know that I appreciate their services very highly, and am very grateful for their fidelity to my interests. I want them to know how I feel toward them. I stand ready at all times to serve them, and will speak to General Garfield on their behalf." He was really moved.

Now, other Presidents have met with as great faithfulness in their subordinates as did President Hayes; other men were better served who had no such feeling about their office force. But here was a man who thought of those things, who considered the other man as much as himself. Mr. Hayes kept his promise absolutely. Whenever he could serve any one of us he did so. He did his best to help me get the back money that was due me from Congress; he wrote to President Harrison in my behalf, besides making the recommendation to General Garfield of which he spoke. Moreover, he asked me many times to visit him. In one of his letters he says:

"Do not forget the old song is still true here,

"The latch-string hangs outside the door
And is never pulled through."

I had no more claim upon him than another. It was just that it was his nature to be hospitable.

After the inauguration, the family went to the home of Secretary Sherman, where several of us called to say good-bye.

It was most unhappily that a printed form came to me from Spiegel Grove. It was dated July 2, 1889, and said:

The friends who have sent telegraphic messages, letters, floral tributes, and newspaper articles, tokens of their regard

SOCIAL LIFE IN HAYES ADMINISTRATION

for Mrs. Hayes and of sympathy with me and my family, are so numerous that I cannot, by the use of the pen alone, within the time it ought to be done, suitably express to all of them my gratitude and thanks.

I therefore beg them to excuse me for sending in this form my assurance of the fullest appreciation of their kindness, and of my lasting and heartfelt obligation to each of them.

At the bottom of the page he had written in his own hand:

All your kind words find their way to my heart.
Thankfully,
RUTHERFORD B. HAYES.

The last time I saw General Hayes was at the Grand Army Reunion in Washington in 1892. That evening I went to call on him at the house on K Street where he was staying. He was at dinner, but he left the table and came up to see me.

"I would rather have a talk with you about old times than eat my dinner," he said, genially. And so we chatted until we said good-bye for the last time.

XIV

GARFIELD AND ARTHUR

THERE was genial good-feeling in the air when James A. Garfield took the oath of office. His nomination had been so much of a surprise—to no man more than to the nominee, who sat in a stupor of surprise while the convention stampeded around him—that not even we of the office force had had time to wear out our interest in talk. There was nothing of the tragedy of disappointed hopes that sometimes makes the departure of a President hard to contemplate. For General Hayes did not believe in second terms, had not coveted one for himself, and was only too glad to retire into private life. The welcome given General and Mrs. Garfield by the retiring White House family was more than the conventional, decent exercise of courtesy. It was marked by real warmth, for the Garfield and the Hayes families were friends.

Garfield was a man of many friends. I think that was the first impression that the new President made upon me. And now I have come to believe that that determined at once much of his strength and his weakness. A hearty and virile force marked him. He was a fine-looking man and well set-up. His eyes were bright gray, his voice was mellow and vibrant. He could not pick up a book or lay down a paper without revealing physical force. He had had a career of many phases—always upward—as a toiling boy, a teacher, a college president, in the army, in Congress. He was a good fellow and companionable. And everywhere the men around him were his friends. His path was marked by them.

They thronged around him now. But political ascendency is a touchstone to display—not the best but the worst. The men who had once been satisfied to spend pleasant evenings with the new President began now to think of place. The White House offices were full of them. I was in charge of the reception-room where men waited, and I had my fill of them. Old friends demanded embassies, post-offices, clerkships. One of them assumed the position of an intimate of the White House and, not satisfied with a comfortable Government berth, pushed himself in past the doors that marked the private domain of the family and took his afternoon siesta upon the most comfortable sofa he could find. The disinterested ones were hurt because they could not chat with the President with the same ease that had marked their visiting with "Jim Garfield." Robert G. Ingersoll was one of these—"Royal Bob" Garfield had christened him. Few were nearer to the President than he. Yet he had to wait long hours in the anteroom. There he was besieged by office-seekers who wished to make use of his supposed interest with the President. Impatience may have colored his caustic answer to one of the applicants. This was a seedy-looking fellow with long, lank locks.

"Colonel Ingersoll," he said, "can't I have your indorsement? You know me. I want a position as chaplain in the army."

Colonel Ingersoll turned a moment from the group of friends with whom he was talking, and eyed him:

"Yes," he said; "I know you. You're a preacher I've met somewhere. You're just the man for my indorsement. You have as little religion as any man I know. You won't hurt any one." And he turned his broad person and chubby face back to the laughing crowd.

But there came a day when the Colonel himself exploded in wrath.

"I'm tired of hanging around here," he said, "kicking my heels in the anteroom. I've had too many games of billiards with Jim Garfield to stand this." And he marched out.

I imagine the President and his wife got as little pleasure out of the restrictions of official life as did Colonel Ingersoll. A shade settled over Mr. Garfield's face, and Mrs. Garfield showed little pleasure in her position. They were people of simple tastes. We had small opportunity to know Mrs. Garfield in the few months before the blow came. She was not strong at any time, was ill during some weeks, and was occupied chiefly in an attempt to secure some privacy for herself and her family, and to organize their life, reserving as much time as possible for the domestic life she loved. The sons of the house—Henry A.,

JAMES A. GARFIELD

GARFIELD AND ARTHUR

James R., and Abram—and little Miss Mollie enjoyed the life as boys and girls always do any novelty. The hours saved from their tutor, Mr. Hawkes, who taught the White House boys in company with Colonel Rockwell's son, were not long enough for the things they found to do.

I find in my diary notes of the usual excitement and suspense accompanying each new administration, the days spent in wondering whether the general shaking-up would be extended to the executive office. On the 5th of March, a day given over to marching bands and curious crowds, the President visited the office. Mr. Rogers, the private secretary of President Hayes, remained a few days to help Mr. J. Stanley Brown, the new and very young private secretary, to organize the office. On the loth of March I was called into the cabinet-room. When I got there I found it was to administer the oath of office for Secretary of War to Mr. Robert Lincoln, whom I had known as a Harvard student in his father's administration.

"Why, hello, Colonel!" he said. And when I replied: "How are you, Mr. Secretary?" he said: "I'm not that yet." But then he took the oath and my mistake was remedied. It seemed good to hear the name Lincoln about the White House. And this Mr. Lincoln had always shown me much of his father's pleasant kindliness. He took this occasion to speak to President Garfield of my long service, my faithfulness to President Lincoln, and his own wish that I might be retained. This brought forth an appreciative answer from the President. So after this, I, for one, felt reassured.

After all, with one exception, there were no changes in the executive office. In fact, even when the spoils system has held unquestioned sway over other Government offices, Civil-Service Reform has usually been observed in the personnel of the President's own office. And that in itself is an interesting point, since the chief appointing power has realized that efficiency can be obtained only where appointments and removals have been separated from party strife.

That question settled, we were next interested in the appointment of those officials with whom we would have most to do. Cabinet-making was in order. The appointment of James G. Blaine, the late Speaker of the House, as Secretary of State, could hardly have surprised any one. In addition to his position on political affairs he was a personal friend of Garfield's. "Gaffy" he was in the intimate conversation of the Blaine family. It was an interesting thing to see these two men, both so vital, so ambitious, so full of attraction for each other and for other men, together. They made much the same impression of virility, of vigor. Garfield has been said to have been better equipped in breadth of view, in actual mental power, than his Secretary of State. But Blaine made up for this in his superior skill in managing men. He had the invaluable faculty of never forgetting a name or a personality. There have been few more interesting personalities in the public life of any nation than James G. Blaine. There was in him something of the Celt, something of the Saxon, something of the poet, much of the orator, that peculiar blend of temperaments in which the elemental power of a crowd goes to the head like wine, but wine which clears the brain, focuses all the faculties into the one masculine passion for domination. The President's power, on the contrary, lay not so much in swaying a crowd— though he was a fine orator—as in logical analysis of a situation rather than in power to force his conclusions on others, in the warmth rather than in the passion of personal attachments.

Scarcely less interesting than the personalities of these two friends was that of Mrs. Blaine. Unpopular with many she was, both at this time and later. An incident of a sort to explain some of the reasons for her unpopularity I will give later on. Strong, dominant, partisan—intensely so—lacking just that balance that would have enabled her to keep back a clever retort or characterization trembling on her tongue when its utterance would be unpolitic, she marched proudly on her way by her husband's side. The brilliant mind and clever tongue have lived chiefly in the shrewd or cutting phrase which—after it had done its work of making an enemy of the public servitor it tagged—passed often into an aphorism of Washington life. The heart whose loyalties or antipathies prompted the phrase has lived in the memory of those who received its devotion.

Much has been said regarding the influence that Mrs. Blaine had over her husband, and, like most such reports, it has probably been exaggerated. But that she shared Secretary Blaine's counsels more than usually falls to the lot of the wives of public men is undoubtedly true. In one of her letters she says, possibly with the almost constantly present license of her humor: "I have been helping Father pick out Gaffy's cabinet." However doubtful it may be that the "helping" went any further than the clarifying influence exerted by the mere act of discussion, or that the "picking" was aimed to do more than to present the premier Secretary's opinions to his Head, it is undoubtedly true that "the Blaines" were to have been a potent influence in the opening administration.

Many persons thought that it was an undue influence. That, of course, is not to be decided until later years when personal feeling is absent. But there were one or two circumstances that came under my observation to show that Secretary Blaine had possibly a closer association with the President than has usually been the case where the President and the Secretary of State have not been in so complete harmony. It was generally believed in the office that Secretary Blaine was kept informed by some member of the President's office force of all events of importance connected with the daily routine—what persons had called, what was their business, and the like. I had myself observed repeatedly that on cabinet days Secretary Blaine would arrive early and be closeted with the President for some time before the rest of the cabinet officials arrived. When the meeting was called, the Secretary of State, instead of going into the room with the President, would come in through the door leading from the main entrance as though he had just entered the White House. In this manner the President and the Secretary of State were able to act in concert on all matters of public policy, more effectively so than if they had not had these conferences. It would naturally be true that they formed a party in cabinet discussions, apart from, and possibly in opposition to, the other members.

I don't know that any one could blame the President for seeking harmony where harmony was to be had. For there has never been a cabinet which contained more elements foreboding dissension. The necessity of considering the "Stalwart" element, disappointed in its desire to make General Grant President, brought men into office who were united to the President only by much-strained party bonds. Conkling's claims to patronage were a fruitful source of strife. The miserable Star Route scandal demanded investigation. And some of the President's former political friends were involved in that. He was beginning to be torn between allegiance to party lines and his duty to the whole country. I know of no administration that promised to be more full of bitterness and strife than that of Garfield.

During the early days of the administration the executive office heard various echoes of the fight that was being waged with Conkling over the New York Custom-House appointment. Whatever may have been the degree to which Secretary Blaine had impressed his own enmity for Conkling—Conkling with his "haughty disdain, his grandiloquent swell, his majestic, supereminent, overpowering, turkey-gobbler strut," as Blaine had labelled him during one of their Congressional tilts—the President evidently thought he was right in refusing to give Conkling's man the place. And the executive antagonism to the New York statesman was reflected in the feeling of many of his subordinates. Conkling-baiters were popular at the White House. I remember on one occasion that Justice Field was inconvenienced by this fact. He came to see the President. He was invited into the private secretary's office and there he waited for almost an hour. Then he became impatient and asked Mr. Stanley Brown when he could see the President. When he was told that the President was engaged he became indignant at having been kept waiting so long. One of the little tempests that so often occur seemed brewing. I tried to smooth things over, but Mr. Brown at first refused to do anything, saying, with natural youthful partisanship:

"The President is talking with Senator Sawyer, who is bearing the burden and heat of the Conkling fight. Just now he is of more importance than any one else!" However, a note was dispatched to Justice Field, so that little matter passed over.

When the news was brought of the resignation of Senators Conkling and Piatt there was great excitement in the office. Newspaper reporters came rushing in to see how we took the news. People darted up to shake us by the hand and say that the country

GARFIELD AND ARTHUR

was well rid of them. Mr. Brown was as exultant as if his nine had won a baseball game.

"Mad boy!" he cried, in parody of Conkling's supposed rage; "take my baseball bat and go right home!"

Now that those "who bore the burden and heat of the conflict" have gone, and those who felt so keenly about it can look back, it is evident how unfortunate was the Conkling quarrel. For it complicated and embittered the few months before President Garfield was shot. It got itself into the Star Route scandal; some men thought that it acted upon Guiteau's sinister folly; and the fruit of it was an ugly suspicion that embittered the whole administration that followed. There was certainly abundant reason for the feeling against Conkling. I suppose there was reason, too, for Conkling's feeling that he had been betrayed; since, for once in his political life, he had sunk his personal animosities for the good of his party when he campaigned for Garfield. And it must have been a pretty bitter thing to have found himself ignored by the administration he had helped to install. There were men who said that the President had made a promise to him which he broke. However that may have been, it was a great fight to see— from the grand-stand.

The preparations for the prosecution of the Government employees who had been defrauding the country of millions by drawing pay for serving spurious mail-routes—in other words, the Star Route criminals— promised to make a great deal of trouble for the

President. The fact that some of the President's personal and political friends were implicated in the Star Route affair made his position a most difficult one. It's a very good thing to have friends. But when they get to fighting they are calculated to make the centre of the rush-line in a football game seem a peaceful retreat.

There was just one thing necessary to draw the attention of the whole country to the evils of the spoils system, with its consequent struggles for patronage. And that thing happened.

It was early in the administration that Charles Guiteau, of Illinois, one of an army of office-seekers, came to Washington to ask the President for a position. He wished to be appointed to the diplomatic service; from St. James to Boma there was no post he did not consider himself capable of filling. I remember very little about him, beyond the fact that he called daily until the 13th of May, when I came into collision with him. On that day he came into the reception-room early in the morning and asked for paper—he wanted to send in a message to the President. I gave him some stationery and he wrote his note and left to go to the Treasury Department. In a short time he was back again, this time evidently under some excitement, asking for paper again.

"The office is supplying you with a good deal of stationery of late," I said, good-naturedly enough, and just for the sake of saying something. As I spoke I handed him some sheets.

"I want some more of the kind I had this morning," he said.

"But that was a sample we happened to have of blue English paper. The man who came after you used up what you left, and we have no more."

"That's the kind I want." He was angry now, and he would have no other. When it was not produced he became still angrier.

"Do you know who I am?" he demanded, impressively.

I was getting a little bit tired of his airs. "I don't know that you are anybody in particular."

Upon this he pulled out a card—I have it to-day—and slapped it down on my desk most dramatically.

"This is my card, sir. I am one of the men that made Garfield President."

"Which one?" I asked, not taking any great pains, I suppose, not to smile. "At least twenty men have already claimed that honor. It would simplify things so much, you know, if we could hit on the one, give him his reward, and end it."

He didn't seem to consider this humorous at all, but turned on his heel and sought a corner of the reception-room, where he sat glowering. Then I consulted with Mr. Brown, thinking I might have made a mistake and that he might really have some claim upon us.

"No, no," said Mr. Brown. "Guiteau is a fraud and ought to be suppressed." It happened that that was the last visit he made, for he was refused admission to the White House on that day.

I don't know what there was in the man's demeanor

that made me notice him particularly, because we were always having to deal with queer characters. But when I went back to my desk I made a rough pencil sketch of him, as he sat in gloomy displeasure, in a diary in which I sometimes made notes of curious or interesting features of White House life. I wrote beside the sketch: "This fellow put on more airs than is usual for a man who is begging for office! Charles Guiteau, of Illinois. One of the men who made Garfield President." I made no pretensions to be an artist—far from it. But it happened that on the 2d of July, when newspaper reporters came rushing to us to learn all they could concerning Guiteau, this pencil scratching of mine was seized upon by the artist of one of the New York papers, and served as the basis of the first picture of Guiteau published after the assassination.

After this incident Guiteau, nothing daunted by having been refused admission, called daily at the White House. Each time he inquired solicitously about the President's health and then went quietly away. There was nothing suspicious in his manner, although the letters he wrote to the President might have warned us all had we not been so accustomed to cranks and their missives.

Even when I met him at the White House the evening before the assassination no thought of danger occurred to me. I had to go to the office to pay the salary of one of the officials who was going away. As I approached the north entrance from the west, Guiteau left it and walked away toward the State

GARFIELD AND ARTHUR

Department. I asked the doorkeeper what he wanted:

"Just to inquire about the President's health," was the reply. I told Mr. Brown this, but the matter ended there.

The fault in the matter, if fault there was, was part of the general system and had obtained for a long time. When applicants put forward their requests for office, the rule was to reply that the applications would be put on file and considered. In the majority of cases there was not the slightest possibility of any position being granted. It was just the usual human method of saving trouble and avoiding a scene. Men often waste months waiting, hanging about the White House and the various departments. If at the outset they were told there was no position for them they might be disappointed for the moment, but the Government would be spared time and expense, and many a life might be saved from shipwreck. It is not often that such devastation is wrought as in the case of Guiteau, but, in a minor degree, millions of men have been injured by just such tactics. Following the event, the usual number of persons came forward with accounts of premonitions of ill to the President at the hands of Guiteau. But the truth was merely that Guiteau had made himself somewhat conspicuous. There was no more reason to think of him as a possible assassin than of many others. I have been told that Secretary Blaine exclaimed, when he first heard the President had been shot: "Guiteau did this!"—having in mind the threatening letters Guiteau had written to the President. But he might have had the same feeling regarding half a dozen others—who finally went quietly home and were never heard of again.

But President Garfield, with his wholesome vigor, his problems of patronage, his proceeding against the Star Route conspirators, his growing sense of lack of harmony in his cabinet, his friendships and his romps with his big, hearty boys, had no time in which to be afraid of possible cranks, and had he been warned he was too much of a soldier to be afraid. And during the final few weeks of his life the illness of Mrs. Garfield occasioned him anxiety. She became ill with a violent fever. When, about nine o'clock on the morning of the 21st of May, Secretaries Blaine and MacVeagh came to see the President, he was not to be found. Messengers searched everywhere for him. At last they dragged him out from behind the curtains of his son's room. He had hidden there to be alone for a few minutes; and tears of weariness filled his eyes.

Mrs. Garfield was ordered away to Long Branch with the children. And on the 2d of July, between eight and nine, the President left to join his family. He was particularly bright, and as happy as a big boy to be getting out of harness for a time.

The office work had hardly begun for the day when "The President has been shot!" flashed through the White House in an instant. While we were still drawn together—hoping, fearing, wondering—a messenger came to say he was on his way home. In an incredibly short time the house was full of people. All of the cabinet officers who could get there and all of the cabinet ladies were waiting. Doctors responded to emergency calls or hurried to the scene on their own responsibility. Orders were issued to admit no one to the White House.

In a wonderfully short time the carriage rolled up to the south entrance. Just before the President was lifted out, he looked up at his office windows where his clerks were gathered and waved his hand to us with a reassuring smile. When he was carried into the hall, high on the shoulders of twelve bearers, he held with his eyes those gathered there and kissed his hand. Mrs. Blaine—impulsive, brilliant, outspoken Mrs. Blaine—went into his room after he was carried in.

"Don't leave me until Crete comes," begged the President, showing, for all his marvellous fortitude, the effort with which he spoke. And then again he said to her: "Whatever happens, take care of Crete." And with tears in her eyes she promised.

In a short time everybody was excluded except by special order signed by the Secretary of War—I have the first card granting admission to the White House that day. In the absence of Mrs. Garfield there was no one to take autocratic charge, as is so necessary in case of serious illness. There was an assemblage of doctors, but some hesitation in organizing the fight against death.

Then followed the agonizing eighty days during which the President fought for life as bravely as he had battled for his country at Chickamauga. The memory of the passion of pity, the suspense, the tenderness, is still vivid in the recollection of the country at large. Public feeling fluctuated with the reports on the bulletin-board. But it can be imagined how much more vehement were the sympathies of the members of his own official household, who waited for tidings separated by but a few partitions from the large room in the southwest corner where the President lay suffering. There were times when it seemed as if his wonderful vitality would conquer—and then every one went around with a bright face. I had a sort of blind faith that he would recover, and there were others, too, about the President who were hopeful. As late as August 17th I told a newspaper correspondent who was getting up an article that I believed the President would pull through.

The afternoon after the President had been shot Mrs. Garfield came back, "frail, fatigued, desperate, but firm and quiet and full of purpose to save," as Mrs. Blaine described her. The President's room and its smaller communicating apartments were then turned, as nearly as was possible, into a hospital; the physician in charge banished all visitors; Mrs. Garfield's own doctor, a prominent woman physician, Mrs. Susan Edson, acted as resident doctor and nurse. Crump, the steward, was a tireless and devoted assistant; he strained himself in lifting and turning the invalid, and has never been well since. Colonel Rockwell, Superintendent of Public Buildings and Public Grounds; General Swaim, the Judge-Advocate General and the President's personal friend, and Colonel Henry mounted guard over the White House, the "kitchen cabinet" the public grew to call them. The campaign against death was on!

It was a fearfully hot July. It was soon evident that the heat would prove a serious obstacle to recovery. To reduce the temperature of the sickroom the cellar of the White House was turned into a refrigerating plant; it was piled high with crates on crates of ice. A pipe led from the cellar to the President's room and conveyed the cooler air in a never-ending stream. Everything that the vigilance of the physicians could compass was done to assist him in his struggle for life.

There was one pathetic feature of the President's martyrdom—his loneliness. From the day when the cordon of physicians closed about him to bear him away to his chamber of suffering he was denied his friends. This, of course, was quite the proper thing to do when there was danger of fever; but, in view of the fact that it was to end fatally, this pain, added to the physical agony of a man who suffered with a heroism that has rarely been equalled, seems heartrending. "Royal Bob" and Blaine were banished with the rest. Those of us who were about the White House know how constantly he begged to see his friends. Crump has often told me how the President begged him to get Blaine to his bedside—Garfield loved Blaine like a brother. And it is easy to understand how, in exhaustion, his heart longed for the glow and vitality of his friend. But a military cordon surrounded the White House, and no one got through. There was one time when even the man's children were sent away.

How his thoughts dwelt where his eyes could not is shown by the letter he wrote his old mother:

> WASHINGTON, D. C., *August* 11, 1881.
> DEAR MOTHER,—Don't be disturbed by conflicting reports about my condition. It is true that I am still weak and on my back, but I am gaining every day, and need only time and patience to bring me through.
> Give my love to all the relatives and friends, and especially to sisters Hetty and Mary.
> Your loving son,
> JAMES A. GARFIELD.
> *Mrs. Eliza Garfield, Hiram, Ohio.*

Beginning strongly and steadily, the handwriting records the fast-ebbing strength until the last word, more a weary driving of the pen than a word, shows only too clearly how soon exhaustion came.

The last view we had of him alive was on the 6th of September, when he was being moved to Elberon in the hope that the air and the sight of the sea might do for him what the doctors could not. We crowded to the windows and were rewarded by seeing the prostrate figure on the stretcher feebly wave its hand—a last token of amity from a man who loved the world and the people in it.

Very little was known in Washington regarding the Vice-President, now become President. And that little identified him with Conkling, the Stalwart element. But Mr. Arthur at once proved himself to be not only a man of kindly and humane feeling, but possessed of a singularly high conception of personal dignity.

Mr. Arthur did not occupy the White House as a dwelling until the 9th of December. In the interim repairs and refurnishing went on vigorously. The President, although Mrs. McElroy, his sister, acted as the nominal feminine head of the household—Mr. Arthur had lost his wife but a short time before his election—had the machinery of entertaining definitely in his own hands. He was a man of artistic taste, with decided ideas in the matter of interior decoration. Every detail of the changes wrought he scrutinized; he made almost daily hours of inspection, and they were more than perfunctory. This was a matter of real importance to him, and he gave it both time and thought.

When the President and his household took possession of the private apartments of the White House it became evident what sharp contrasts there are in the social standards held together under a political organization in this big country of ours. During the preceding administrations the White House had been full of vigorous, overflowing life, often of the noise and laughter and romping of young children. The Presidential family had been in essence democratic, with a certain respect for the opinions of the masses that had placed them where they were. Their private life they had often conceived as belonging, in some part, to the public, their children were the nation's children, their social functions but rendered to the public what was the public's due.

With Mr. Arthur a change took place. Whether, as I have said, he was influenced by the cruelties the public had heaped upon him, or whether it was his own idea of the fitness of things, a sharp line was drawn between the public and the private life of the White House. The newspaper impertinence which made a great furore over the flowers daily heaped before a woman's portrait in the President's own room—only to be discomfited to find the portrait that of the dead wife—may have confirmed his determination that the public should have as little as possible of his family life. Mr. Alan Arthur was a student at Princeton. But little Miss Nellie was brought up in as scrupulous retirement as the most exacting Continental requirements for the education of a young girl would have dictated. We saw occasionally a sweet-faced little girl walking or driving by her father's side, or with him in the halls. As far as I know she was photographed only once, when, during one of her brother's visits home, he put the little sister, of whom he made a great pet, on a pony and had a picture taken then and there. Once or twice, during the last years of her father's administration, she appeared for a short time at an afternoon reception, dressed in schoolgirl cashmere or muslin. But that was about all the public knew of the family life of President Arthur.

As for the social life, it again had two distinct phases. Mr. Arthur never lost sight of the idea that the White House was in truth the court of the American people. Nothing could have been more scrupu-

CHESTER A. ARTHUR
From a photograph by C. M. Bell.

lous than his observance of set form and precedent in the formal social entertaining at which he presided. There was no possibility of heartburning over the question of precedence at state functions. Mr. Arthur gave the subject careful consideration, and then organized a system of precedence that was always maintained. That being done, he knew how to take such entertaining out of the realm of mere political necessity, where it had always been and, by his exquisite courtesy, tact, and skill in keeping the conversational ball rolling, make them social functions as well.

But for his private affairs he demanded the liberty that any citizen may command. He had his own intimate personal friends and those he preferred to entertain in his own way. There were reports that the White House, so staid and so orderly during the day, was gay and even convivial at night. The President loved late hours; he loved to entertain his friends in the small private dining-room, made, under his direction, into a snugly luxurious setting for one of the best of bon vivants and raconteurs; there was special attention paid to the viands that were consumed and the wines that were drunk. All this, of course, was magnified by popular report. I remember there used to be a little tradition among us that the President had installed a "property basket" filled with official-looking documents with which he was wont to enter the office for a delayed business appointment, and on which he made no more progress than the embroidery which some ladies like to reserve for occasions when a touch of graceful domesticity is to be produced.

The truth is, the President was not a generally popular man. He was always courteous in his official relations—with just a suggestion of distance. We had all become accustomed to the sort of a man who, whether he were aware of it or not, desired the approval of the men he met as sincerely as any would be Congressman stumping his district three days before election. But there must have been something haughty in President Arthur's belief in himself, something of "The king can do no wrong." He took no trouble to contradict rumors or to ingratiate himself with those who had started them. He was a handsome man, generous in his proportions—overtopping most men and as straight as a rail—with a suggestion of richness in the coloring of his hazel eyes and fresh-colored face. As there are always social cliques and rivalries, there were various reports about him.

The fact is, Washington was not accustomed to just the type of man that President Arthur represented. Because he was somewhat of an epicure, because he believed that social life and the arts are factors in life of equal importance with political primaries, his recreations were exaggerated out of all proportion and his statesmanship ignored.

It is for other people to discuss these topics. I can say this, however. An administration that had promised to be torn by dissension, the prey of spoilsmen, defeated by the quarrels of Republicans among themselves, somehow straightened out into order, efficiency. That is the sort of thing that becomes apparent to an office force. Somehow everything that had to be done was done, without regard to party or personal friendship. Conkling, Star-Routers, Navy—all could affirm that. There were no more colloquies between disaffected officials behind screens; there was no more question of the President's policy being dominated by this politician or that. Whoever did it, there was more work done, more order created, less of political scandal during Arthur's administration than the White House has often witnessed.

But it was not recognized at the time. If the tragedy of Garfield's administration called attention to the evils of the spoils system, this administration and the election that followed showed to what an extent the dissemination of scandal could be permitted among supposedly decent people. And it was only when a life or so had been hurt by it that the evil was stayed.

One little incident stands out in my mind in the midst of other very different things. An old colored man journeyed to the White House to see the President. While he was waiting to be received he told me all about how he had belonged to the family of President Arthur's wife, and how he had carried his "little Miss" in his arms to school. I suppose he expected that the President would bestow upon him a pension for life because of the service, but I never heard of this having been done.

It was but natural that President Arthur should have wanted the renomination. It would have been authoritative assurance that his choice for the Vice-Presidency was not a mere political chance. But he made singularly little effort to obtain the nomination in 1884. I suppose he was under the impression that his administration might speak for him; there was again something almost haughty in the way he disregarded some of the powerful politicians, with their following. I know personally that John A. Logan was waiting for an audience with the President. Had it been given he would have turned over to him the votes he controlled—and Arthur might have received the nomination instead of Blaine. But the President steadfastly refused to see him—and the votes went elsewhere. The only time I ever saw Mr. Arthur show any personal emotion was when he said good-bye to his office force at the coming in of Cleveland. Then he was very evidently moved.

THE END

www.ingramcontent.com/pod-product-compliance
Lightning Source LLC
LaVergne TN
LVHW051039080426
835508LV00019B/1598